TALES OF OLD SINGAPORE

The glorious past of Asia's greatest emporium

Iain Manley

"Of all the places in the Orient, the most cosmopolitan is Singapore, the gateway to the Far East; the one city which everyone encircling the globe is forced to visit, at least for a day."

George Hamlin Fitch, 1913

Tales of Old Singapore

ISBN-13: 978-988-18667-3-8

Design by Frank Zheng

China Economic Review Publishing (HK) Ltd publishing for Earnshaw Books, Hong Kong

Acknowledgments

Nobody learns history as an entirely linear narrative. Instead, we assemble it ourselves, from the bits and pieces we pick up along the way. This is a book of pictures, photos, eyewitness observations and historical bric-a-brac - bits and pieces picked up, loosely organised and where necessary explained. Like memory, it has holes. Important events, places and people may have been left out or understated, but obscure slices of daily life have also been brought to life, and it is my hope that the vanished world of old Singapore bustles again within these pages.

The attributions in the body of the book are collected in a full bibliography at the back. I believe all items are out of copyright or within the bounds of fair usage, but should you find any uncited or incorrectly attributed material, please inform us so that appropriate changes can be made in future editions.

My thanks to David Fyfe, Derek Sandhaus, Claire van den Heever, Heather Manley, Graham Earnshaw, Frank Zheng, Lim Hui Sin and Ian Pringle for their guidance and encouragement, and for delving with me into Singapore's past.

Iain Manley

Please visit us at TalesOfOldChina.com,
the website from which this book sprang.

An Old Singapore Chronology

3rd century: Early Chinese accounts appear of Singapore, or *Pu Luo Chung*.
13th century: The port of Temasek, or Singapura, is founded by Srivijaya prince Sang Nila Utama.
1320: Mongols send mission to obtain elephants from *Long Ya Men* (Dragon's Teeth Gate), believed to be Keppel Harbour.
1414: Temasek incorporated into the Sultanate of Malacca.
1511: Portuguese take Malacca; Temasek becomes a part of the Sultanate of Johor.
1613: Portuguese burn down a trading outpost at the mouth of Singapore River.
1819, January 29: Stamford Raffles and William Farquhar establish trading post in Singapore for the British East India Company.
1826: Singapore becomes part of the Straits Settlements with Malacca and Penang, under the control of the East India Company.
1832: Singapore becomes the capital of the Straits Settlements.
1839: First Singapore-built vessel is launched.
1845: *The Straits Times* is established.
1860: Telegraph opened between Batavia (Jakarta) and Singapore.
1867, April 1: Straits Settlements become a crown colony of British Empire.
1869: The Suez Canal opens.
1877: The Chinese Protectorate is established by William Pickering. Rubber is introduced to Malaya.
1879: Singapore Club, Chamber of Commerce and Exchange Building are opened.
1887: The Raffles Hotel is built.
1906: Singapore dollar notes are introduced.
1915, February 15-25: Sepoys rebel during the Singapore Mutiny.
1923: Johor Causeway opens.
1941, December 10: *HMS Prince of Wales* and *HMS Repulse* are sunk by Japanese bombers.
1942, February 15: The British surrender to the Japanese Imperial Army. Occupation of Singapore, renamed *Syonan*, begins.

Sir John Anderson, Gov. of Straits Settlement, 1904-11

1945, August 14: Japan capitulates. A month later, the British return to Singapore.
1946, April 1: Straits Settlements dissolved.
1948: Rubber plantations and tin mines in Malaya are destroyed by communists. State of emergency declared.
1950, December 11-13: 18 people killed during the Maria Hertogh riots.
1956, June: David Saul Marshall appeals to the UK for full self-government, resigns upon failure. Lim Yew Hock becomes Chief Minister.
1959, March: Lim Yew Hock gains full self-government for Singapore.
1959, May: People's Action Party (PAP) wins general election and Lee Kuan Yew becomes first Prime Minister.
1963: Singapore declares unilateral independence from Britain and joins the Federation of Malaysia.
1965, August 9: Singapore expelled from the Federation of Malaysia. The Republic of Singapore is established.

Leaders of Singapore

Residents

Major-General William Farquhar	
Dr John Crawfurd	
Governors of the Straights Settlements	
Robert Fullerton	Nov 1826 – Nov 1830
Robert Ibbetson	Nov 1830 – Dec 1833
Kenneth Murchison	Dec 1833 – Nov 1836
Sir Samuel George Bonham	Nov 1836 – Jan 1843
Col. Major-General William John Butterworth	Aug 1843 – Mar 1855
Edmund Augustus Blundell	Mar 1855 – Aug 1859
Major General Sir William Orfeur Cavenagh	Aug 1859 – Mar 1867
Major General Sir Harry Ord	Mar 1867 – Nov 1873
Sir Andrew Clarke	Nov 1873 – May 1875
Sir William Jervois	May 1875 – Apr 1877
Major General Edward Archibald Harbord Anson (Acting)	Apr 1877 – Aug 1877
Sir William Cleaver Francis Robinson	Aug 1877 – Feb 1879
Major General Edward Archibald Harbord Anson (Acting)	Feb 1879 – May 1880
Sir Frederick Weld	May 1880 – Oct 1887
Sir Cecil Clementi Smith	Oct 1887 – Aug 1893
William Edward Maxwell (Acting)	Aug 1893 – Feb 1894
Sir Charles Mitchell	Feb 1894 – Dec 1899
Alexander Swettenham (Acting)	Dec 1899 – Nov 1901
Sir Frank Swettenham	Nov 1901 – Apr 1904
Sir John Anderson	Apr 1904 – Sep 1911
Sir Arthur Young	Sep 1911 – 17 Feb 1920
Sir Laurence Guillemard	17 Feb 1920 – Jun 1927
Sir Hugh Clifford	Jun 1927 – Feb 1930
Sir Cecil Clementi	Feb 1930 – Nov 1934
Sir Shenton Thomas	Nov 1934 – Feb 1942 & Sep 1945 – Apr 1946
Governors of Singapore	
Sir Franklin Charles Gimson	Apr 1946 – Mar 1952
Wilfred Lawson Blythe (Acting)	Mar 1952 – Apr 1952
Sir John Fearns Nicoll	Apr 1952 – Jun 1955
William Goode (Acting)	Jun 1955 – Jun 1955
Sir Robert Brown Black	Jun 1955 – Dec 1957
William Goode	Dec 1957 – Jun 1959

Government House, now called the Istana, not long after it was completed in 1869

Introduction

Old Singapore was the greatest emporium in Asia, and perhaps the world – a city organised like an immense department store, in which you could buy and sell just about anything. Established by a nation of shopkeepers, it welcomed anybody who came to work or trade: opium dealers, prostitutes and coolies, along with merchants and tradesmen from Europe and every corner of the East. Some made vast fortunes, and the self-made man was accorded the utmost respect; others were worn down by hard labour, killed at sea by pirates or assassinated by triad thugs. But for over a century, Singapore boomed. And although few ever thought of it as home, their individual pursuit of riches built an Asian city of unrivalled diversity and prosperity, and eventually invented a nation.

The settlement was an immediate, almost overnight, success. Founded in 1819 on the ruins of Temasek, capital of Malay king Parameswara, it had a population of 5,000 and trade tallying up to eight million Spanish dollars by 1821. In 1825, its population

Chinatown from Pearl's Hill, 1847

surpassed 10,000 and trade reached $22 million, exceeding that of the much older British port of Penang.

Its rapid success is usually attributed to its perfect location and near-perfect founder, Stamford Raffles. The Strait of Malacca is the natural conduit for ships sailing to and from China and Japan, and Singapore, at its narrow southern entrance, has a natural deep-water harbour. Geography alone might have been enough, but also Raffles made Singapore a free port in a time when the Dutch, colonial masters of much of the region, levied onerous duties on ships not flying their flag. *Laissez faire* British rule was so popular that the Dutch unsuccessfully blockaded their own harbour at Malacca to prevent the merchants there – a diverse mixture of Arabs, Armenians, Jews, Indians, Malays and Straits Chinese – from moving to Singapore.

Raffles did not preside over the pell-mell rush to settle the island. Instead, he installed Colonel William Farquhar as Resident and returned to Bencoolen, where he was Lt. Governor. Farquhar was perhaps too easygoing: he turned a blind-eye to slavery, licensed vice and allowed houses to be built in an area Raffles had reserved for commerce. When Raffles returned in 1822, he had Farquhar removed and carefully reorganized the town, but Singapore soon sprawled beyond even Raffles' optimistic expectations.

Immigrants started arriving from further afield – some convicts, others coolies, soldiers, merchants or administrators – and by 1827, Chinese residents had overtaken Malays to become the settlement's

Raffles Hotel in the early 1900s. Singapore's last tiger was shot underneath its billiards hall.

largest ethnic group. In 1860, Indians knocked Malays into third place. Singapore also became a part of the Straits Settlements, created in 1824 after Britain and the Netherlands divided the region between themselves along roughly the same lines that separate Malaysia from Indonesia today.

Responsibility for the Straits Settlements and its diverse peoples fell on governors appointed by the British East India Company, who often knew little about the region and were primarily concerned with the bottom line. In 1850, despite widespread lawlessness caused by powerful criminal societies, 12 police officers were responsible for some 60,000 residents. Singapore's administrators also ignored the importance of cultural differences – the misnomer 'native' was regularly applied to Chinese, Indians and Malays alike – and not a single British official could speak Chinese.

In 1867, two years after Singapore became a Crown Colony, the Suez Canal opened, drastically reducing the length of the journey from Europe to Asia. The world's shipping was, at the same time, exchanging sails for steam and steamships needed bigger, better equipped ports, where they could take on coal. In 1877, rubber was introduced to the island and just 30 years later, when automobiles reached a mass market for the first time, Malaya was the largest producer of plantation rubber in the world. Singapore prospered. Between 1873 and 1913, the volume of trade handled at the port increased eight fold, making it the second busiest port in the world after Liverpool.

It became a modern, industrial, hugely unequal and exceptionally cosmopolitan city. Its *towkays* and *tuans* – wealthy Chinese merchants and Europeans, respectively – lived lives of giddy excess. Europeans started work at 10am and finished at 4:30pm, with an hour for lunch. Their copious free time was filled with tennis, cricket, horse racing, rugby and fives, as well as tea dances and banquets served by liveried servants in the breeze of punkah fans pulled by men labelled 'peons'. Guests at the city's luxury hotels, the world's first global tourists, were waited on by teams of servants without which they "couldn't get on" and between whom they couldn't distinguish. Tigers were a menace – until the last was killed underneath the billiards room at Raffles Hotel in 1921 – but nobody worried much, because man-eaters seemed more interested in "the flesh of coolies" than Europeans. Coolies, on the other hand, had more than tigers to worry about. Mostly indentured labourers from southern China or India's east coast, they lived short, hard

lives away from home, and many died at the Paupers' Hospital from malnutrition or opium addiction.

Despite minor setbacks during WWI and the Great Depression, life continued gaily until WWII, when the Japanese defeated the British and began a brutal occupation of the island. A month after the Japanese surrender, the British returned a diminished power - beatable, exhausted by war and guilty of incredible hubris - to a colony in a mess. The people of Singapore began to call for independence, and Britain agreed to gradually grant it. In 1946, the Straits Settlements was dissolved. Singapore became a separate colony and limited elections were held, but just two years later, British troops began battling Communist guerrillas on the Malayan Peninsula. It was not until 1955 that the next step was taken towards self government, including almost complete control over domestic policy. In 1956, the Chief Minister, David Marshall, went to London to appeal for full independence. He was rejected. Frequent riots had brought the legitimacy of his party's rule into question and the British felt that, without their continued involvement, communists might take over the island. Marshall resigned. His replacement, Lim Yew Hock, cracked down on leftwing parties and, in 1959, Singapore was granted full internal self-government under the leadership of Lee Kuan Yew.

Lee believed that Singapore's future lay in a united Malaya and, despite strong opposition, achieved his goal in 1963, when Malaya, Singapore, Sabah and Sarawak merged, creating the Federation of Malaysia. It was not to last. Malays feared Chinese dominance and bloody race riots broke out. On August 9, 1965, the short lived federation ended with the expulsion of Singapore. Lee received the news with tears, but declared the full independence of Singapore, and Singapore would - in time, under his guidance - prove exceptional. It would become the world's greatest port city and a beacon for the potential of Asia.

Much that was colourful about old Singapore was, inevitably, left behind. It has been almost 200 years since Raffles left the island's shores, but, despite the intervening busts and even more transformative booms, Raffles would still recognise his creation, and probably approve. Singapore is still a well-administered free port - it is still charting the course on which he set it. I hope that you will enjoy tracing its journey as much as I have.

Iain Manley
October 2010
Shanghai

Singapore Ahoy!

From Glimpses into Life in the Far East *by JT Thomson, 1864*

"Singapore ahoy!" exclaimed the man at the mast as the white houses and shipping rose above the horizon while we were abreast of the large red cliffs. We hailed the "Queen of the East" with no small pleasure…In the foreground, busy canoes, sampans, and tongkangs bore their noisy and laughing native crews about the harbour. The stately "Hyacinth" showed the pennant amongst numbers of English merchantmen. Hundreds of Chinese junks, and Malay prows, lay further in shore. Behind these, stretched a sandy beach, glistening in the sun, and overhung by the graceful palm trees, the glory of Singapore planters. In the centre of the landscape was Government Hill, with its verdant lawns and snug bungalow; and at its base were the warehouses and mansions of the merchant princes. Behind these was to be seen the comely undulating background, alternately covered with the mighty forest trees, and gambier and pepper gardens.

"Captain Whalley seemed to be swept out of the great avenue by the swirl of a mental backwash. He remembered muddy shores, a harbour without quays, the one solitary wooden pier jutting out crookedly, the first coal-sheds erected on Monkey Point…He remembered the things, the faces, and something besides—like the faint flavour of a cup quaffed to the bottom, like a subtle sparkle of the air that was not to be found in the atmosphere of to-day."

Joseph Conrad, The End of the Tether, *1902*

The Smiling Peace of the Eastern Seas

From Joseph Conrad's 1899 novel Lord Jim. *Jim, the protagonist, is thought to have been inspired by a resident of Singapore.*

The hospital stood on a hill, and a gentle breeze entering through the windows, always flung wide open, brought into the bare room the softness of the sky, the languor of the earth, the bewitching breath of the Eastern waters. There were perfumes in it, suggestions of infinite repose, the gift of endless dreams. Jim looked every day over the thickets of gardens, beyond the roofs of the town, over the fronds of palms growing on the shore, at that roadstead which is a thoroughfare to the East,—at the roadstead dotted by garlanded islets, lighted by festal sunshine, its ships like toys, its brilliant activity resembling a holiday pageant, with the eternal serenity of the Eastern sky overhead and the smiling peace of the Eastern seas possessing the space as far as the horizon.

Tanjong Katong, Singapore.

"Singapore was the last jumping-off place from civilisation into a world as terrible as it was beautiful, rich and savage and cruel beyond belief, of land and seas still unexplored where even the mighty Royal Navy sent only a few questing warships, and the handful of white adventurers who voyaged in survived by the speed of their keels and slept on their guns."

George MacDonald Fraser, Flashman's Lady

Singapore's Population

1821: 5,874	1891: 181,602
1824: 10,683	1901: 226,842
1830:13,634	1911: 303,321
1840: 35,389	1921: 418,358
1849: 52,891	1931: 557, 745
1860: 81,734	1947: 938,144
1871: 96,087	1960: 1,646,400
1881: 137,722	1965: 1,886,900

"The history of Singapore is written mainly in statistics."

Sir Richard Winstedt, Malaya and its History, *1948*

"The present population of Singapore amounts to 30,000; of which there are only 7229 females. Of Europeans, there are 105 males and 36 females; Malays, 5122 males, 4510 females; Chinese, 12,870 males, 879 females; Klings, 2246 males, 102 females. The rest are Bugis, Balinese, Bengalese, Negroes, Javanese, Arabs, &c.; with a few Indo-Brittons, Armenians, &c."

Howard Malcom, Travels in South Eastern Asia, *1839*

"The United States Treasury Department gives the trade of Singapore (April, 1898) as $210,000,000, consequently larger than that of all Japan ($195,000,000), or all of the Dutch East Indies ($147,000,000). Only the Empire of China ($277,000,000) rivals this little British port in the total of its commerce."

Poultney Bigelow, The White Man's Rule in Singapore, *1899*

The Handiest City Ever

From Two Years in the Jungle *by William Temple Hornaday, 1885*

Singapore is certainly the handiest city I ever saw, as well planned and carefully executed as though built entirely by one man. It is like a big desk, full of drawers and pigeon holes, where everything has its place, and can always be found in it.

For instance, around the esplanade you find the European hotels and bad enough they are, too; around Commercial Square, packed closely together, are all the shipping offices, warehouses, and shops of the European merchants; and along Boat Quay are all the ship chandlers. Nearby, you will find a dozen large Chinese medicine shops, a dozen cloth shops, a dozen tin shops, and similar clusters of shops kept by blacksmiths, tailors, and carpenters, others for the sale of fruit, vegetables, grain, "notions," and so on to the end of the chapter. All the washerwomen congregate on a five-acre lawn called Dhobi Green, at one side of which runs a stream of water, and there you will see the white shirts, trousers, and pajamas of His Excellency, perhaps, hanging in ignominious proximity to and on a level with yours. By some means or other, even the Joss houses, like birds of a feather, have flocked together at one side of the town. Owing to this peculiar grouping of the different trades, one can do more business in less time in Singapore than in any other town in the world.

The Singapore Stone

A year after Singapore was established, a large slab of inscribed rock was found near the banks of the Singapore River. The inscription, now thought to be in Sanskrit or Old Javanese from sometime between the 11th and 13th centuries, could not initially be deciphered, and in 1843, during a widening of the river's entrance, the stone was blown to pieces. Only a small fragment now remains. Abdullah bin Abdul Kadir, better known as Munshi Abdullah, described the first attempts to decipher the inscription in The Hikayat Abdullah, *first translated into English in 1849.*

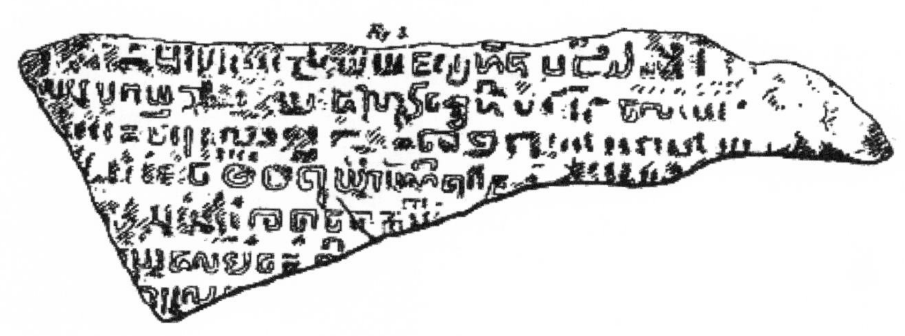

The rock was smooth, about six feet wide, square in shape and its face was covered with a chiselled inscription. But although it had writing this was illegible because of extensive scouring by water. Allah alone knows how many thousands of years old it may have been. After its discovery crowds of all races came to see it. The Indians declared the writing was Hindu but they were unable to read it. The Chinese claimed that it was in Chinese characters. I went with a party of people, and also Mr Raffles and Mr Thomsen, and we all looked at the rock. I noticed that the lettering was rather like Arabic, but I could not read it because owing to its great age the relief was partly effaced.

The Lion City

From British Malaya *by Sir Frank Swettenham, 1906*

Singa is Sanskrit for a lion, and *pûra* for a city, and the fact that there are no lions in that neighbourhood nowadays cannot disprove the statement that Sang Nila Utâma saw, in 1160 or thereabouts, an animal which he called by that name—an animal more particularly described by the annalist as "very swift and beautiful, its body bright red, its head jet black, its breast white, in size rather larger than a he-goat." That was the Lion of Singapûra, and whatever else is doubtful the name is a fact; it remains to this day, and there is no reason why the descendant of Alexander should not have seen something which suggested a creature unknown either to the Malay forest or the Malay language.

"In the year 1703 I called at Johor on my way to China, and the King of Johor treated me very kindly and made me a present of the island of Singapore, but I told him it could be of no use to a private person, though a proper place for a company to settle a colony on, lying in the centre of trade, and being accommodated with good rivers and safe harbours, so conveniently situated that all winds served shipping both to go out and come into these rivers."

Captain Alexander Hamilton, 1727

Rough on You, Ducky

From The Brisbane Courier, *Aug 30, 1884*

In the prime of hot July, my husband,
When the heat is rising fast,
When the coolie softly pulling
Paddles out a burning blast;
When the skies are lurid yellow,
When our rooms are 'ninety-three,'
It were best to leave you, ducky –
Rough on you but best for me.

Naming the Lion City

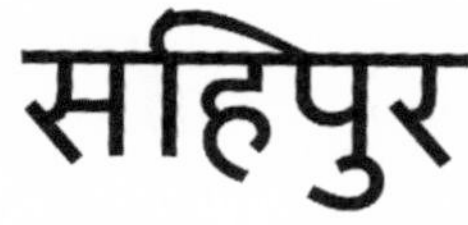

Singapura, Sanskrit

سيڠاڤورا

Singapura, Malay Jawi script

新加坡

Sin–ka–pho in Hokkien and *xīnjiāpō* in Mandarin, also sometimes

星嘉坡 or 星加坡

昭南島

Shōnantō, during Japanese occupation

சிங்கப்பூர்

Ciṅkappūr, Tamil

Nothing Scanty, Feeble or Pale!

In The Golden Chersonese and the Way Thither *by Isabella Bird, 1883*

It is hot—so hot!—but not stifling, and all the rich-flavored, colored fruits of the tropics are here—fruits whose generous juices are drawn from the moist and heated earth, and whose flavors are the imprisoned rays of the fierce sun of the tropics. Such cartloads and piles of bananas and pine-apples, such heaps of custard-apples and "bullocks' hearts," such a wealth of gold and green giving off fragrance! Here, too, are treasures of the heated, crystal seas—things that one has dreamed of after reading Jules Verne's romances. Big canoes, manned by dark-skinned men in white turbans and loin-cloths, floated round our ship, or lay poised on the clear depths of aquamarine water, with fairy freights—forests of coral white as snow, or red, pink, violet, in massive branches or fern-like sprays, fresh from their warm homes beneath the clear warm waves, where fish as bright-tinted as themselves flash through them like "living light." There were displays of wonderful shells, too, of pale rose-pink, and others with rainbow tints which, like rainbows, came and went—nothing scanty, feeble, or pale!

A Free Port

From Trade and Travel in the Far East *by G.F. Davidson, 1846*

Singapore is a free port; and vessels of all kinds and from all nations come and go, without paying one penny to Government in any shape. All that is required of them is to give in a list of the goods they either land or ship. This regulation is intended to enable the authorities to keep a correct statement of the trade of the place; but it is, I am sorry to add, often evaded by ship-masters and their consignees, who seem to think that no trade can be profitably conducted without a certain portion of mystery attaching to it.

One Large Warehouse

From Celebrated Travels and Travellers *by Jules Verne, 1881*

Singapore was simply one large warehouse, to which Madras sent cotton cloth; Calcutta, opium; Sumatra, pepper; Java, arrack and spices; Manilla, sugar and arrack; all forthwith despatched to Europe, China, Siam, &c. Of public buildings there appeared to be none. There were no stores, no careening-wharves, no building-yards, no barracks, and the visitors noticed but one small church for native converts.

The Paper War

In 1818 Stamford Raffles, then Lt. Governor of Bencoolen, calculated that two thirds of East Indies' trade was controlled by Holland and much of the remainder by local chieftains bound to trade exclusively with the Dutch. He believed that a free port, in the right place, could break this monopoly.

William Farquhar, a Scottish army major, agreed. Farquhar had been removed from his position as Resident of Malacca when the Dutch took it over in 1818. Raffles and Farquhar received little encouragement from Calcutta or London, because of concerns that a British threat to Dutch trade might cause conflict closer to home. With scant room to manoeuvre, the two eventually struck on a narrow passage between the Malacca Strait and South China Sea at Rhio, but were prevented by Dutch ally Tengku Abdul Rahman, Sultan of Johor. The men then decided to sail, in Raffles' words, to "the site of the ancient city of Singapura."

They arrived on Jan 29, 1819 and were met by the Temenggong, a powerful Malay chieftain who had fled there after unsuccessfully attempting to have Tengku Long, the Sultan's older brother, installed on Johor's throne. On Feb 1, Tengku Long arrived and was recognized by Raffles as the Sultan of Johor and Singapore. In this capacity, he allowed for the creation of a trading settlement at Singapore. Both he and his brother later told the Dutch they had agreed under duress, but the deal was done. Raffles left the next day and Farquhar became Singapore's first Resident.

Then a paper war began. Singapore was largely defenceless, but the only Dutch challenge to the new settlement was legal. In the age before steamships and telegraphs, letters from Asia to Europe often took as long as six months to arrive and, despite strong words, the Dutch achieved little. It was 1924 before an agreement was reached, by which time Singapore was already a thriving British port.

"The Dutch possess the only passes through which ships must sail into the Archipelago, the straits of Sunda and Malacca; and the British have now not an inch of ground to stand upon between the Cape of Good Hope and China, nor a single friendly port at which they can water and obtain refreshment."

Stamford Raffles, 1818

The Rat City

In Raffles of Singapore *by Emily Hahn, 1946*

It is alleged that "Singapura" in one of the Indian tongues means "Lion City" but the only animals on the island were rats, who made up in number what they lacked in size. So many were they that, far from fearing the cats that came ashore off the ships, they killed them by ganging up, until Raffles offered a bounty of one *wang* – i.e., two cents ha'penny for every dead rat brought to him. Thousands were killed in the following days, until there was not one rat left. Then Raffles and the Malaccans turned their attention to the thousands of centipedes which were doing their little bit to render the Lion City revolting. The bounty method disposed of them as well. And now this scrub-covered piece of unattractive land was ready, the stage was set, and the curtain rose on the drama of Raffles's Eastern empire.

The Want of More Ground

From a letter written by William Farquhar to Stamford Raffles in 1820

Nothing can possibly exceed the rising trade and general prosperity of this infant colony. One of the principal Chinese merchants here told me, in the course of conversation, that he would be very glad to give five hundred thousand dollars for the revenues of Singapore five years hence. Merchants of all descriptions are collecting here so fast that nothing is heard in the shape of complaint but the want of more ground to build on.

Raffles' True Memorial

From Raffles *by R. Coupland, 1926*

Singapore, then, the Queen of British Malaya, is Raffles' true memorial. He has been forgotten at times in London; he has never been forgotten there. Raffles Quay, Raffles Place, Raffles Museum, Raffles Hotel – everywhere the city cries out his name. And on the border of Raffles Plain, in front of him the azure roadstead with its crowd of ships from all the world, behind him the green peninsula with its millions of contented villagers, stands Raffles' statue, watching for all time over his political child. There, if anywhere on earth, his spirit lingers, at peace, his dream fulfilled.

A statue of Stamford Raffles in front of the Victoria Theatre

Col. William Farquhar

"It irks me as a good Hollander to have to admit it, but it would have been an obstruction to world trade if Singapore had belonged to the Netherlands Indies."

P.H. van der Kemp, 1814

The Jackson Plan

In 1822, Stamford Raffles resigned his post as governor at Bencoolen. He was ill, had recently lost three children and was on his way home, but paid a final visit to Singapore. Excited by the success of the colony, Raffles was also annoyed by Farquhar's administration of its growth. Contrary to orders, the Resident had sold gambling, opium and liquor licenses, allowed unplanned construction to the north of the river and turned a blind-eye to slavery. Although so ill that he thought he might die in Singapore, Raffles had Farquhar removed and, during an productive nine month stay, gave engineer Lt. Philip Jackson instructions for the reorganisation of the town.

The Jackson Plan divided Singapore into ethnic 'campongs' – today's Chinatown, Little India and Arabia – laid its roads out in a strict grid, at a prescribed width, and allotted land to a European town, government buildings, a military cantonment, religious sites, a botanic garden and a Commercial Square – today's Raffles Place. It stipulated that houses must have a verandah "open at all times" to the street – the city's characteristic five-foot way – and went as far as outlining a standard appearance for the front of homes, permanently leaving on Singapore the mark of Raffles' rational, Enlightenment mind.

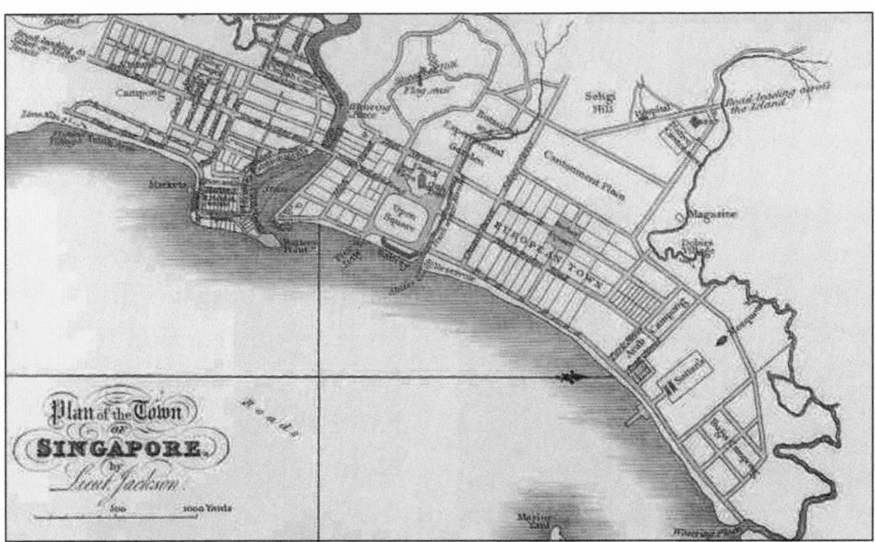

The Jackson Plan, also sometimes called the Raffles Plan

The Foot-way Riot

From Around the World through Japan *by Walter Del Mar, 1904*

The houses in the business quarters of Singapore project over the footway, and are supported by columns and arches so as to form a veranda or colonnade such as is still to be seen at Piccadilly Circus. Here the shopkeepers, mostly Chinese, were accustomed to display their wares to the inconvenience of foot-passengers not engaged in shopping. A regulation to keep the foot-way clear led to a riot; and whether there was a formal rescission or not, the Chinamen practically gained the day, as they still continue to occupy the foot-way with their goods to the inconvenience of pedestrians.

John Little department store, seen here in the late 19th century at Raffles Place, first opened in Singapore in 1845.

Lounging Natives of Half a Dozen Nationalities

In the Otago Witness, *May 1, 1901*

The covered verandah-like footways, which are the only sidewalks, are filled with varied litters of goods displayed for sale; the rest of the narrow space is crowded by men squatting in groups smoking and gossiping, by men asleep, by men bartering with stony-faced shopkeepers, by pariah dogs nosing and searching, by stray goats, by squalling children, naked, dirty and happy, and by lounging natives of half a dozen nationalities.

"Architecturally considered, Singapore has little to boast of except solidity and uniformity. With but few exceptions the buildings are all Chinese, and perfectly innocent of style. It is a two-story town throughout, solidly built of brick, plastered over, and painted a very pale blue or light yellow. There is a remarkable scarcity of the tumbledown, drunk, and disreputable old buildings so essential to the integrity of all other large cities."

William Temple Hornaday, 1885

10,000 Souls to Legislate For

From a letter written by Stamford Raffles to T. Murdoch, Dec 4, 1822

I am now busy in allotting the lands and laying out the several towns, defining rights, and establishing powers and rules for their protection and preservation. I have been a great deal impeded, but the task, though an arduous and serious one, is not one that I find unpleasant. What I feel most is want of good counsel and advice, and a sufficient confidence in my own experience and judgment to lay down so broad and permanent a foundation as I could wish. I have already upwards of 10,000 souls to legislate for, and this number will, I doubt not, be increased during the next year. The enterprise and activity which prevails are wonderful, and the effects of free trade and liberal principles have operated like magic. But, that the past prosperity of the place may not prove ephemeral, it requires that I be the more careful in what I do, for the future: for if the past, under all our uncertainty of possession, has so exceeded my expectations, what may not be calculated upon hereafter, when our possession is considered secure, and when British capital and enterprise come into full and fair play?

Victoria Theatre in the early 20th century

Fine Buildings and Foul Odors

From George Hamlin Fitch's The Critic in the Orient, *1913*

Singapore has a population of over three hundred thousand people; it has a great commercial business, which is growing every year; it already has the largest dry dock in the world. Its bund is not so imposing as that of Hongkong, but it has more public squares and its government buildings are far more handsome. As Hongkong owes much of its splendid architecture and its air of stability to Sir Paul Chator, so Singapore owes its spacious avenues, its fine buildings, its many parks, its interesting museum and its famous botanical gardens to Sir Stamford Raffles, one of the British empire-builders who have left indelibly impressed on the Orient their genius for founding cities and constructing great public enterprises. Yet, Singapore, with far more business than Manila, is destitute of a proper sewer system, and the streets in its native quarters reek with foul odors.

The Most Thriving Colony in the East Indies

In Benjamin Morrell's A Narrative of Four Voyages, *1832*

For the short period it has been in existence, Singapore is, without an exception, the most thriving colony which the British have in the East Indies; being admirably situated for all the purposes of trade; and is, in fact, a centre depot for the commerce of the Chinese and Javanese seas...Among the valuable articles brought to this market are tortoiseshells, pearls, and pearl-shell, ambergris, gold-dust, edible birds' nests, birds of paradise, minerals, biclie-de-mer, shells, pepper, coffee, sugar, hemp, indigo, many valuable gums and drugs, precious woods, many of which are readily purchased by the British merchants who have establishments at this place...Within the last ten years, this place has increased and flourished beyond all calculation. An Indian village of forty or fifty bamboo huts has given place to a splendid well-built little city.

Orchard Rd. Railway Bridge, late 19th century

> "Singapore, growing up in the midst of ancient island colonies, under the very noses of Batavia and Manila, welcomed the people and the products of all its rivals, and within the lifetime of one man took rank among the few great seaports of the world."
>
> *Poultney Bigelow,* The White Man's Rule in Singapore, *1899*

EASTERN ARTICLES.	From	To
Nankeens, short, per corge	$—	$—
Oil, cocoanut, per picul	4	4½
Opium, Patna, per chest		1000
Benares, "		1000
Malwa, "	—	—
Pepper, black, per picul	5	5½
white, "	7½	8
long, "	6¼	7
Piece goods, Bengal, sunnahs, per corge	36	40
Mahmoodies, per corge	30	32
Gurrahs, per corge	22	26
Baftahs, "	22	24
chintz of 12 cubits, per corge	15	17½
chintz of 10 cubits, "	10	14
Madras, moorees, white, "	22	25
blue, "	30	35
salempires, blue, per corge	30	40
brown, "	28	32
handkerchiefs, per corge	30	100
kolamhories, "	20	45
kambayas, "	12	13
bugis sarungs, "	18	40
Bali cloths, "	5	7
Batick hdkfs. "	14	24
Ratans, per picul	1¼	2
Sago, pearl, in cases, per picul	2¼	2½
Salt, Siam, per coyan	22	24
Saltpetre, per picul	7	8
Sapan wood, Manilla, per picul	¼	2
Siam, per picul	2	2½
Silk, raw, China, junk, 72 cts.	200	250
Canton, No. 2, 100 cts.	300	325
No. 3, 95 cts.	285	290
Spices, nutmegs, per picul		
cloves, per picul	20	30
mace, "	40	49
Spirits, arrack, per gallon	30	40 ct.
Stick lac, per picul	13	15
Segars, Manilla, per 1000	6	7
Sugar, Java, per picul	5¾	7
Siam, first sort, per picul	6½	7
Manilla, per picul	5½	6
Sugar-candy, per picul	12	13
Tin, Banca, "	15	16
Tin, Straits, per picul	$14½	$15
Tobacco, Java, 40 baskets	200	250
China, per picul	19½	22
Tortoise-shell, "	1000	1600
Turmeric, "	2¼	3

WESTERN ARTICLES.	From	To
Ale, Hodgson, per hogshead	40	45
Anchors and grapnels, per picul	11	14
Bottles, English, per 100	4	
Books, &c.	—	—
Canvass, per bolt	10	12
Copper nails and sheathing, per picul	40	42
Cordage, per picul	12	14
Cotton, "	11	13
Cotton twist, No. 16 to 36, per picul	50	55
No. 38 to 70, per picul	80	
No. 40 to 80, "	85	
Earthenware		
Flints, per picul	1½	2
Glassware		
Gunpowder, canister, per 100lbs	30	40
Hardware, assorted		
Iron, Swedish, per picul	5½	6
English, "	3¼	3½
nails, "	8	10
Lead, pig, "	5½	6
sheet, "	6	7
Oilman's stores, "	—	—
Patent shot, per bag	3	3½
Paints, black	—	—
green	—	—
white lead	—	—
Provisions, beef, per tierce	33	35
pork, per barrel	28	30
biscuit, per picul	6½	7
flour. "	8	9
Piece goods, Madapolams, 25 yds. by 32 in., per piece	2½	3½
Piece goods, imitation Irish, 25 yds. by 36 in., per piece	$2½	$3
long cloths, 38 to 40 yds. by 34 to 36 in., per piece	7	7¾
38 to 40 yds. by 38 to 40 in.,	7	8
" by 44 in.	7	9
" by 50 in. } " by 55 in. }	9	12

A list of the goods traded at Singapore divided into Eastern and Western Articles, from A Narrative of Four Voyages *by Benjamin Morrell, 1832*

Alexander Laurie Johnston

A description of Singapore's first European trader, remembered in the naming of Johnston's Pier, from An Anecdotal History of Old Times in Singapore *by C.B. Buckley, 1902*

It was during 1820, or more probably in 1819, that Mr. Alexander Laurie Johnston came to Singapore. When he left Singapore in 1841, he said, in reply to an address that was presented to him, that he had been longer in Singapore than any one he left behind him, and that he had witnessed its rise from little better than an uninhabited jungle. He was a native of Dumfrieshire in Scotland, and...enjoyed the especial friendship, and was much in the confidence, of Sir Stamford Raffles, who placed his name, as we shall see, at the head of the first list of Magistrates who were appointed to administer the laws of the infant Settlement. The letters and notes addressed by Sir Stamford to Mr. Johnston bear ample testimony to the frequency and benefit with which his advice and assistance were sought in all matters affecting the interests of the Settlement. In almost every public transaction, Mr. Johnston was at the head. He was one of the first Trustees of the Raffles Institution, he was the first Chairman of the Chamber of Commerce, and the precedence which was always accorded to him on all public occasions showed the respect and esteem with which he was regarded and the kindliness of his manners and disposition. The natives and Chinese readily sought his advice, and in cases of dispute his decision was as much respected as a judgment of the Court, so highly was he appreciated by them. It was said that no Court was required in his day, as no one thought of going to law while there was Mr. Johnston to determine the matter, and all disputes of importance were laid before him as a matter of course. He was liberal and hospitable in the extreme, and in the earliest cash book that seems to have been opened when he commenced business here, the first entry to his personal debit is as follows:—"A. L. Johnston,— Paid subscription for release of a female European slave, $10." He established the house of A. L. Johnston & Co., the pioneer European mercantile firm in the place. He died in Scotland in 1850.

Alexander Laurie Johnston

The Most Sparkling Fable of the East

A Narrative of Four Voyages, *Benjamin Morrell, 1832*

From the dawn of day until sometime after sunrise, the most sparkling fable of Turkey, Persia, or all the East is fully realized in Singapore. Every leaf, and flower, and spray, and blade of grass, is gemmed with dewdrops of extraordinary clearness and purity; which have imbibed so much of the vegetable fragrance, that when they begin to exhale in the increasing warmth of the solar ray, the whole atmosphere is filled with the most delightful perfumes, and every passing zephyr scatters grateful odours from its wings.

A Huge Irish Stew

In The Capital of a Little Empire *by John Dill Ross, 1898*

To people of moderate or small incomes Singapore is robbed of all its attractions, and the air, to them is hot and gritty, and is full of sneaps and snubs. The climate of Singapore is healthy, but very trying and monotonous. It has an abominable trick of making the whole place steam and smoke, in a misty way, like a huge Irish stew, and to a poor man, on a wet day, Singapore looks like a "wan waste of weary waterbutts," causing the wretched man to get liverish and swear at the place variously.

"**Compound**, an inclosure, a yard. This is an Anglo-Indian sophistication of the Anglo-Indian *campong*, representing the Malay word kampong, kampung, in early mention (1631, Haex) also written campon. The sophistication is like that which appears in *godown*, sometimes, *godon*, for *godong*, *gadong*, a Malayan word which is excluded from this paper as being of Indian origin."

Charles Payson Gurley Scott, The Malay Words in English, *1897*

The Colloquial Malay

From Around the World through Japan *by Walter Del Mar, 1904*

The colloquial Malay commonly spoken by all Asiatics in Singapore is different from the Sundanese dialect of Java, and the Roman characters used to express the sounds have other values. For the sound of *oo* in cuckoo, *u* is employed instead of *oe*. The *g* and *t* is always hard, and final *k* is not sounded, while *j* and *ch* are pronounced as in English. It is necessary to acquire a limited vocabulary in order to communicate with the Malay or Chinese jinricksha *(Kreta Hong Kong)* men or the Indian hack-gharry *(Kreta Seiva) syces*. *Pergi* (pronounced piggy), drive to, or go to; *berhenti* (pronounced brenti), stop; *tuan* (or the Indian word *sahib*), meaning Mr.; *Punchaus Sahru*, Raffle's Hotel; and *Punchaus Besar*, the Hotel de l'Europe, were phrases learnt the first day, and, as Royds frequently remarked, were "jolly useful."

The Abode of Chinks, Dinks and Stinks

From Looking for Luck *by James Redfern, 1930*

Singapore – the melting pot of the East! Wherever I had met white men I had heard tales of this strange polyglot city; the abode, some said, of Chinks, Dinks and Stinks; others, less cynical, told me: "You'll like it, or you'll hate it, but if you go there you'll never forget it." In Malay, the word Singapura means "City of the Lion," but behind the British lion's back a good deal goes on which he knows nothing about, as I was soon to learn…We went everywhere in the less reputable quarters, the gambling hells, the opium dens, the brothels in Malay Street, Japanese wrestling matches, the Chinese theatre, eating-houses, cockfights, enjoying all the more sordid delights of the city. I dare say I saw more of Singapore than the planters and government officials who had been in the city for ten years.

"Well, thinks I, if Singapore, the fleshpot of the Orient, can't supply my urgent needs, and give me enough assorted depravity in three weeks to last the long voyage home, there's something amiss; just let me shave and change my shirt, and we'll stand this town on its head."

George MacDonald Fraser, Flashman's Lady

Bound Hand and Foot by Commerce

From Some Glimpses into Life in the Far East *by J.T. Thomson, 1864*

Subjects of nations at war are friendly here, they are bound hand and foot by the absorbing interests of commerce. The pork-hating Jew of Persia embraces the pork-loving Chinese of Chinchew. The cow-adoring Hindoo of Benares hugs the cow slaying Arab of Juddah. Even the Englishman, proud yet jolly, finds it to his interest to unbend, and associate with the sons of Shem, whether it be in commerce, in sports, or at the banquet.

South Bridge Rd, 1900s

A Great, Heathenish City

From The Golden Chersonese and The Way Thither *by Isabella Bird, 1883*

The native streets monopolize the picturesqueness of Singapore with their bizarre crowds, but more interesting still are the bazaars or continuous rows of open shops which create for themselves a perpetual twilight by hanging tatties or other screens outside the sidewalks, forming long shady alleys, in which crowds of buyers and sellers chaffer over their goods, the Chinese shopkeepers asking a little more than they mean to take, and the Klings always asking double. The bustle and noise of this quarter are considerable, and the vociferation mingles with the ringing of bells and the rapid beating of drums and tom-toms—an intensely heathenish sound. And heathenish this great city is. Chinese joss-houses, Hindu temples, and Mohammedan mosques almost jostle each other, and the indescribable clamor of the temples and the din of the joss-houses are faintly pierced by the shrill cry from the minarets calling the faithful to prayer, and proclaiming the divine unity and the mission of Mahomet in one breath.

An Honorable Commerce

From Howard Malcolm's Travels in South Eastern Asia, *1839*

The commerce of the countries in and around the China Sea, would form an important and interesting theme for the political economist. From the elegant and civilized Chinese to the wildest tribes which roam the interior of the most unknown islands, all are animated and benefited by an honorable commerce, which existed for ages before the European found his way into these seas. The savage Batta collects camphor; the Daya and Harafoora gather diamonds and gold; the Solu dives for pearl; the Malay explores his lonely shores for edible birds' nests, or gathers the nutmeg and the clove, or sweeps the shore for tripang and agar-agar; the Bugis acts both merchant and mariner, bearing these gatherings from port to port; the Sumatran furnishes pepper for all the world; the more civilized Japanese smelts ores, and constructs articles of elegant utility; the still more refined Chinese gives impulse to the whole by his luxury and his capital; while the Western world shares the precious commodities, and returns the thousand productions of more perfect sciences and arts. This vast, populous, and favored portion of the earth, is that which the ancients, even so late as the time of Constantine, regarded as untenable by man; inhabited only by satyrs, centaurs, headless monsters, and human pygmies.

"The angles of our old friend Euclid offer a fitting simile for three races here. The right angle, symbolical of the Englishman we trust—square; the acute angle liken unto the Kling—sharp, but without much in it; whilst the obtuse angle may properly represent John Chinaman—blunt, not very graceful, but capacious and sturdy withal."

J.H.M. Robson,
People in a Native State, *1894*

A Perfect Commercial Babel

In The Blockade of Quedah *by Captain Sherard Osborn, 1860*

The creek separated Singapore into two distinct parts. The one was purely commercial, with its bazaar and market-places, its native town, and overflowing stores, a perfect commercial Babel, where, if a confusion of tongues would induce men to cease building temples to the goddess of wealth, they would have taken ship and fled the spot. There was an energy, a life, a goaheadism about everything, that struck me much; everybody was in a hurry, everybody pushing with a will. The boatmen condescended to tout for passengers, and were blackguards enough, we heard, to occasionally rap the passengers over the head if they objected to pay them the fare—a proceeding the passengers in other parts of India often reverse by illtreating the cowardly boatmen; then came along a crowd of half-naked Chinese, staggering under some huge bale of goods, and working with a will which would put London porters or Turkish hammels to the blush; a crowd of black and oily Hindostanees, screeching like jackdaws over a stack of bags of sugar, and Arabs, Englishmen, Jews, Parsees, Armenians, Cochin-Chinese, Siamese, half-castes, and Dutchmen, each struggling who should coin dollars fastest; and as my coxswain, a Gosport boy, expressed himself, on his return from making some humble purchases—"Well, I thought they were a smart set on Common Hard, sir, but blest if they don't draw one's eyeteeth in Sincumpo!"

Market Scene, Singapore

Fowl	ayam	鷄
Free	bibas; merdheka	自主
Friend	kawan	朋友
Frog	katak; kodok	田蛤仔
From (places)	deri	對
From (a person)	deripada	對
Front, in	di-hadapan	頭前
Fruit	buah	菓子
Fry	goring	煎
Fulfil, to	sampaikan; gnapi	應驗
Full	pnoh	滿
Further	lbeh jauh	較遠
Game	permainan	遊戲
Gamble	main judi	賭博
Gaol	pnjara; jeil	監舘
Garden	kbun	花園
Gardener	tukang-kbun	園丁
Gate	pintu	門
Gather, to (pick up)	pungut	挽
Gather together, to	kumpol; kampongkan	收
Gentleman	tuan	先生

Although the majority of Singapore's population was Chinese, the island's lingua-franca was Malay. The Triglot Vocabulary, *1891, compiled by William G. Shellabear, was a popular English, Malay and Chinese phrasebook.*

The Raffles Institution

In 1823, towards the end of his very busy final stay in Singapore, Raffles established the Singapore Institution, along the lines of an institution outlined here, in his 1821 essay titled "On the Advantages of Affording the Means of Education to the Inhabitants of the Further East". Now called the Raffles Institution, it is Singapore's oldest school.

The objects of such an institution may be briefly stated as follows: — *First.* To educate the sons of the higher order of natives. *Secondly.* To afford the means of instruction in the native languages to such of the Company's servants and others as may desire it. *Thirdly.* To collect the scattered literature and traditions of the country…Thus will our stations become not only the centers of commerce and its luxuries, but of refinement and the liberal arts. If commerce brings wealth to our shores, it is the spirit of literature and philanthropy that teaches us how to employ it for the noblest purposes. It is this that has made Britain go forth among the nations, strong in her native might, to dispense blessings to all around her. If the time shall come when her Empire shall have passed away, those monuments of her virtue will endure when her triumphs have become an empty name. Let it still be the boast of Britain to write her name in characters of light.

Raffles Institution, Singapore.

Chitties

From John Fairlie's Life in the Malay Peninsula, *1892*

The bankers, or *chitties*, as they are called, are men who have come from Bengal. These men borrow money from the banks of Singapore, and let it out at a greater interest that they pay to the banks…These chitties are very miserly, and keep their money in boxes, on which they sleep. They do not own the houses which they occupy, but rent them from the Malays. Perhaps fifty of them will live in one room. All business is done on credit. If you enter a bazaar and call for refreshment, you do not pay for it in cash, but simply give what is called a chit, or note, which is redeemed on a certain date. If you take a cab for a drive through the place, the payment is made in the same way; you give the driver a chit, and tell him where and when to call for the cash. These chits are also used as currency, since they pass from one merchant to another at a discount. Of course chits are not accepted from people unless they are in a position to pay them. If one has no occupation he gets another to sign for him. When a debtor is brought before the court, if he can prove that he has no occupation or means of livelihood, the debt is cancelled. With such a system the courts are kept pretty busy.

Slightly Grilled and Smelling Horribly

In Accounts of Singapore Life *by G.M. Dare, Jun 1856*

While shooting on the jungly swamps beyond the racecourse and the Hindoo cremation grounds last Friday, I came across the remains of three dead bodies on an open plain amid the swamps, evidently belonging to a class of Hindoos who burn their dead, first covering the corpses with wood, to which they set fire. Two of the bodies were charred to cinders, but on the third the fire had apparently gone out, and there he was, only slightly grilled and smelling horribly. Wild pariah dogs had run away with one of his legs and part of his thigh, of which I found the bones some distance off, partly devoured.

(63) Tamil Actors.

The Most Attractive among All the Nationalities

From The Golden Chersonese and the Way Thither *by Isabella Bird, 1883*

Among the twelve thousand natives of India who have been attracted to Singapore, and among all the mingled foreign nationalities, the Klings from the Coromandel coast, besides being the most numerous of all next to the Chinese, are the most attractive in appearance, and as there is no check on the immigration of their women, one sees the unveiled Kling beauties in great numbers.

An Idolatrous Procession

In Voyages around the World *by Andrew Carnegie, 1884*

We saw in Singapore our first lot of Hindoos, moving about the streets like ghosts, wrapped in webs of thin white cotton cloth, which scissors, needle, or thread have never defiled. The cloth must remain just as it came from the loom; no hat, no shoes, their foreheads chalked, or painted in red with the stamp of the god they worship and the caste to which they belong. They are a small, slight race, with fine, delicate features.

I went out for a stroll before retiring, and hearing a great noise up the street, followed and came up with a Hindoo procession. The god was being paraded through the Hindoo portion of the town amid the beating of drums and blowing of squeaking trumpets. The idol was seated in a finely decorated temple upon wheels, drawn by devotees, many of whom danced wildly around, while others bore torches aloft, making altogether a very gorgeous display. Priests stood at each side performing mysterious rites as the cortege proceeded. It was my first sight of an idolatrous procession, and it made a deep impression upon me, carrying me back to Sunday-school days, and the terrible car of Juggernaut and all its horrors.

The Singapore Mutiny

Less than a year after WWI broke out in Europe, there was a mutiny of the Indian troops, or sepoys, garrisoned at Singapore. The first shots – fired at 3:30pm on Feb 15, 1915, the second day of Chinese New Year – were initially mistaken for firecrackers. Residents soon realized that about 800 men of the 5th Indian Light Infantry – mainly Punjabi Muslims – and nearly 100 men of the Malay Guides Mule Battery had rebelled, leaving Singapore almost entirely defenceless.

The soldiers murdered their commanding officers and then split into two groups. One hundred seized Tanglin Barracks, where 309 German POWs were incarcerated; the others moved towards the town, killing indiscriminately. At the bungalow of Colonel E.V. Martin, British commander in Singapore, the mutineers were held until morning. A force of irregulars, police and miscellaneous troops – including Allied marines – had been mustered overnight and, after a pitched battle, the leaderless mutineers scattered. Fighting continued for only a few days more, but it was weeks before the last mutineers, who had fled into the jungle, were rounded up. The mutiny left about 40 soldiers and civilians dead.

The sepoys' motives were mostly religious. The 5th were due to be transferred to Hong Kong, but had been told by Kassim Ali Mansoor, a middle-aged coffee shop owner, and Nur Alam Shah, an imam at a Singapore mosque, that they were in fact being shipped to Turkey, where they would be forced to fight against fellow Muslims and the leader of their faith, Sultan Mehmet V. Mansoor and Shah were later linked to the Ghadar Party, an Indian organisation trying to incite general mutiny against British rule. The 5th had also been guarding German POWs, who had so successfully exaggerated their alliance with the Ottoman Empire that many sepoys believed Kaiser Wilhelm II had converted to Islam. But when the sepoys arrived at Tanglin barracks to free their supposed comrades, only 35 took the opportunity to escape. Most considered mutiny dishonourable and, later, some even took up arms against the 5th.

Forty-seven mutineers were executed, many of them publicly. On Mar 26, 22 were shot by firing squad against the wall of Outram Prison, in front of an estimated 15,000 spectators.

> "Had the trouble started at midnight, as scheduled, instead of at 3 o'clock in the afternoon, a general slaughter would have ensued."
>
> New York Times, *May 2, 1915*

Mutineers being executed against the wall of Outram Rd Jail, 1915

> "You do not be anxious about anything...Germany has become Mohammedan. His name has been given as Hajji Mohammed William Kaiser German. And his daughter has been married to the eldest Prince of the Sultan of Turkey who is heir to the throne after the Sultan. Many German subjects and army have become Mohammedans. If God so wishes, it will be the increase of Mohammedan's faith."
>
> *From a 1915 letter written by sepoy Mohammed Ali to his mother*

The Leader of the Mutineers

By "The Wife of an English Official" in The Times, *Mar 26, 1915*

He is a native officer, an awful-looking beast with a fierce face and wuffy black beard. He had been wounded in the shoulder and his picturesque white draperies and turban were soaked with blood. The English officer says he is a very bad character and hopes he will be shot or hung. At present he is in a cell just below us and is spending his evening reciting the Koran in a monotonous sing-song voice.

The Seat of Piracy

From The Pirate's Own Book *by Charles Elms, 1837*

A glance at the map of the East India Islands will convince us that this region of the globe must, from its natural configuration and locality; be peculiarly liable to become the seat of piracy. These islands form an immense cluster, lying as if it were in the high road which connects the commercial nations of Europe and Asia with each other, affording a hundred fastnesses from which to waylay the traveller. A large proportion of the population is at the same time confined to the coasts or the estuaries of rivers; they are fishermen and mariners; they are barbarous and poor, therefore rapacious, faithless and sanguinary. These are circumstances, it must be confessed, which militate strongly to beget a piratical character.

A Malay sampan

Human Skulls Rolling About on the Sand

From The Hikayat Abdullah *by Abdullah bin Abdul Kadir, 1849*

All along the shore there were hundreds of human skulls rolling about on the sand; some old, some new, some with hair still sticking to them, some with teeth filed and others without. News of these skulls was brought to Colonel Farquhar and when he had seen them he ordered them to be gathered up and cast into the sea. So the people collected them in sacks and threw them into the sea. The Sea Gypsies were asked "Whose are these skulls?" and they replied "These are the skulls of men who were robbed at sea. They were slaughtered here. Wherever a fleet of boats or a ship is plundered it is brought to this place for a division of the spoils. Sometimes there is wholesale slaughter among the crews when the cargo is grabbed. Sometimes the pirates tie people up and try out their weapons here along the sea shore."

A Chinese City

From Travels in South Eastern Asia *by Howard Malcolm, 1839*

In going through one part of the town, during business hours, one feels himself to be in a Chinese city. Almost every respectable native he sees is Chinese; almost every shop, ware-room, and trade, is carried on by the Chinese; the hucksters, coolies, travelling cooks, and cries common in a great city, are Chinese. In fact, we may almost call Singapore itself a Chinese city; inasmuch as the bulk of the inhabitants are Chinese, and nearly all the wealth and influence, next to the British, is in their hands.

"The largest proportion of charges of felony is found on the side of the Chinese: who, in the main, at this island, are little better than the refuse population of China."

Maj. James Low, 1841

"The Chinese junks bring annually to this part of the world, from six to eight thousand emigrants, ninety-nine-hundredths of whom land without a sixpence in the world beyond the clothes they stand in."

G.F. Davidson, 1846

Lee Kuan Yew Gets a Caning

From The Singapore Story *by Lee Kuan Yew*

In my final year, 1935, I came first in [junior] school and won a place in Raffles Institution, which took in only the top students... I enjoyed my years in Raffles Institution. I coped with the work comfortably, was active in the Scout movement, played cricket and some tennis, swam and took part in many debates. But I never became a prefect, let alone head prefect. There was a mischievous, playful streak in me. Too often, I was caught not paying attention in class, scribbling notes to fellow students or mimicking some teacher's strange mannerisms. In the case of a rather ponderous Indian science teacher, I was caught in the laboratory drawing the back of his head with its bald patch.

Once I was caned by the principal. D.W. McLeod was a fair but strict disciplinarian who enforced rules impartially, and one rule was that a boy who was late for school three times during one term would get three strokes of the cane. I was always a late riser, an owl more than a lark, and when I was late for school the third time in a term in 1938, the form master sent me to see McLeod. The principal knew me from the number of prizes I had been collecting on prize-giving days and the scholarships I had won. But I was not let off with an admonition. I bent over a chair and was given three of the best with my trousers on. I did not think he lightened his strokes. I have never understood why Western educationists are so much against corporal punishment. It did my fellow students and me no harm.

A Peranakan girl

A Malay boy

Sold to Work in a Tin Mine

The statement made by a sinkeh – the Chinese word for a new arrival in Singapore – called Chew-Ah-Nyee, after he was arrested and beaten for rioting when he refused to board a ship. From William Pickering's 1877 Report on Kidnapping Senkehs.

I come from the prefecture of Kow-Chew-foo, and am a School-master. I was engaged in teaching, when about the 24th of the 11th moon, Chiang-See and Kuai-leong told me that they could get me plenty of work at Singapore as a clerk, and that the wages here were very good; I believed them, and was put on board a junk and brought to this place, where I was sold to a shop, chop "Hiap-tye." We came on shore on the 2nd of the 1st moon, there were 90 men from my district, the strong men were sent to saw-yards I believe, but I was sold as a "little pig" being weak. This morning I was being taken to a boat with many others, I don't know where they were taking us to, but we heard that the place is 11 or 12 days' sail from this, and that we had to work in tin mines; of course we refused to go to another country, as we had understood Singapore to be our destination, and I can't work as a miner. On our way to the boat we refused to proceed, so the Khehtows struck us and threatened us with the Mandarins; they did call the Government Officials who struck me and my companions, and we were afterwards brought here. Chiang-see and Kuai-leong paid my passage here, but it was on the understanding, that when I got employment at Singapore, I should repay them. I never thought of being sold to work in tin-mines. All the money I have received is $1 in copper to buy clothes with.

Hoo Ah Kay

Hoo Ah Kay moved to Singapore from Canton in 1830, at the age of 15, to help his father run a general store. He learnt to speak English impeccably and by 1840 had used it to make his father's business, Whampoa & Co, a supplier to the Royal Navy. After his father's death, Hoo expanded the company, investing in plantations and opening an ice house as well as a bakery. Whampoa & Co became well known in Singapore and Hoo became known as "Mr Whampoa". When the Straits Settlements became a crown colony in 1867, the Governor nominated him a non-official member of the ruling Legislative Council and later an extraordinary member of the Executive Council. Hoo was the only Chinese person to ever achieve this position and was said to rub peppermint essence into his nostrils to stay awake during the councils' ponderous meetings. He was also simultaneously consul for Russia, China and Japan in Singapore, but was perhaps best known for his Chinese garden, which was open to the public during the Chinese New Year. In 1867, he was appointed a companion of the Order of St. Michael and St. George and four years later, at the age of 64, he died.

"That the most active, industrious, and enterprising race in the Eastern world should be regarded as a source of weakness, rather than of strength to a community, implies, *prima facie*, a certain degree of mismanagement."

Laurence Oliphant, 1859

The Chinese Clerk

In The Brisbane Courier, *Mar 26, 1884*

The Chinese clerk, who speaks and writes English, having acquired these accomplishments at Raffles school, which is under English mastership, has much better prospects. He is more intelligent, has greater perseverance and a wonderful aptitude for business. Very often he commences life on a salary of $15 per month, often *much* lower, and in a short time he makes money, then launches into business on his own account, and blossoms into one of our millionaires. I know three firms here where the head Chinese clerk has much more money than his master, and I can mention five Chinese who now own fleets of big steamers officered by Europeans.

Dear Old Whampoa

From A Sailor's Life Under Four Sovereigns *by Admiral Henry Keppel, 1899*

Whampoa was a fine specimen of his country, and had for many years been contractor for fresh beef and naval stores. His generosity and honesty had long made him a favourite. He had a country house, and of course a garden; also a circular pond in which was a magnificent lotus, the *Victoria regia*, a present from the Regent of Siam...The huge lily grew splendidly, and bore leaves over eleven feet in diameter... When in blossom, Whampoa gave sumptuous entertainments to naval officers: although our host, he would not eat with us, but sat in a chair, slightly withdrawn from the table. At midnight, by the light of a full moon, we would visit this beautiful flower, which faced the moon and moved with it until below the horizon. Amongst other pets he had an orang-outang, who preferred a bottle of cognac to water.

Dear old Whampoa's eldest son was sent to England for education, and while there became a Presbyterian. When I was in Singapore years after, the young man returned, and had the assurance to reappear before his father, fresh and well, but minus a tail, and consequently was banished to Canton until it regrew and he consented to worship the gods of his fathers.

A Chinese merchant's home

The Chinese Towkay

In People in a Native State *by J.H.M. Robson, 1894. Towkay (头家) was Hokkien for head of the household.*

After a time one discovers that there are a number of very good fellows among the Chinese, especially amongst those who bear the honoured prefix Towkay to their name. There is the mining Towkay, the contracting Towkay, the trading Towkay, the fishing Towkay, and a host of other little Towkays, in fact any Chinaman who has risen in the world called himself a Towkay.

Coming here as coolies under advances, never forgetting the birth-place and people they have left, with the speculative, practical, toiling attributes born within them, with nothing to lose and everything to gain, is it after all anything so very wonderful that some rise and blossom out into wealthy Towkays?

The personal peculiarities of a Towkay are not numerous; one appears to be that he must needs let his nails grow to the length of an inch or more…This is an outward indication that the hands are not soiled by manual labour, but from personal observation I should imagine that this elongated little finger is kept as an—er—toothpick, say.

Another little peculiarity of my good friend, the Towkay, is the painful and audible habit he has of clearing his throat on arrival, during a conversation and even at meal times. He can hardly keep clock-work in his throat, but from the sounds one might suppose that about ten main springs had all broken at once, and he was doing his best not to swallow any of them.

A Good and Orderly Citizen

In British Borneo *by W.H. Treacher, 1891*

It is not, I think, sufficiently borne in mind, that a very large proportion of the Chinese there are of the lower, I may say of the lowest, orders, many of them of the criminal class and the scourings of some of the large cities of China, who arrive at their destination in possession of nothing but a pair of trousers and a jacket and, may be, an opium pipe; in addition to this they come from different provinces, between the inhabitants of which there has always been rivalry, and the languages of which are so entirely different that it is a usual thing to find Chinese of different provinces compelled to carry on their conversation in Malay or "pidgeon" English, and finally, as though the elements of danger were not already sufficient, they are pressed on their arrival to join rival secret societies, between which the utmost enmity and hatred exists. Taking all these things into consideration, I maintain that the Chinaman is a good and orderly citizen and that his good qualities, especially as a revenue-payer in the Far East, much more than counterbalance his bad ones.

The Tiger Balm King

In LIFE, *Jul 21, 1941*

Singapore is a city for the rich. The wealth of the world's tin and rubber pours through it. But the most picturesque rich man is neither a white man nor a tin king. He is a Chinese manufacturer of a patent medicine called Tiger Balm which is sold all through the Indies as a cure-all. The Tiger Balm King is Aw Boon Haw and his brother is named Par. Their flamboyant estate outside Singapore is named Haw Par Ville (Chinese first names come last). Aw Boon Haw is a joke in Singapore but his name is reverenced in China's capital of Chungking to which he has sent large amounts of cash for the war against Japan. He drives a tiger-striped car to advertise his balm and is suspected of all kinds of illicit enterprises.

Letter Writers

The men and women who came to Singapore looking for work were largely illiterate, but needed to communicate with the people back home, usually in China. Letter writers made this possible, and reported on the births, loves, deaths and marriages of complete strangers for a reasonable fee. They also drafted contracts, wrote poems and helped clients calculate foreign exchange rates. Almost entirely Chinese, letter writers' calligraphy was often beautiful, and often of solely ceremonial importance.

The Peranakan

The Peranakan or Straits Chinese were amongst the earliest inhabitants of Singapore. Mostly from Malacca, where there had been a sizeable Chinese community since the 15th century, the Peranakan rose to be Singapore's most successful traders, often working as intermediaries between the British, Malays and merchants from China. The community maintained a number of China's traditions, including its religions and festivals, but the Peranakan spoke Malay and adopted Malay dress. Intermarriage was also common, particularly of Peranakan men to Malay women. The men were referred to as babas and the women as nonyas, which led to a third name for the community, the Baba-Nonya.

A Peranakan bridesmaid

Baba Tan Tock Seng

Tan Tock Seng was born in British-occupied Malacca in 1758. When the colony was returned to the Dutch in 1818, Tan followed the former British Resident, William Farquhar, to his new command at Singapore. Tan sold fresh food and, as the settlement grew, accumulated enough capital to set himself up as a middleman. The business of Singapore was moving goods and money between the ships of different races and Tan, a Peranakan, spoke Malay at home, could muddle through in Hokkien and had learned a little English in Malacca. He prospered and spent his wealth generously, first on a hospital for Chinese paupers, for whose funerals he also paid, then on the construction of Thian Hock Temple, which became a centre of Chinese social life in Singapore. In 1844, Tan was the first Asian to be made the Straits Settlements' Justice of the Peace – a role of great importance as Singapore began its battle with Chinese secret societies – a position he held until his death in 1850.

The Tan Tock Seng Hospital

From Sunny Singapore *by John Angus Bethune Cook, 1907*

It is a pleasure to write of the Tan Tock Seng Hospital 'for the sick of all nations,' though its many wards, with about one thousand beds, are used mostly by Chinese patients...It was founded by Mr. Tan Tock Seng, the father of the late Consul for Siam, Mr. Tan Kim Ching, who also gave large sums of money, as his grandson, Mr. Tan Boo Liat, and other members of his family have done. Many other Chinese merchants have contributed towards the erection and maintenance of the buildings. The hospital is staffed and worked by Government along with a committee of Chinese gentlemen... Mr. Teo A. Hok, of Foochow, went with me on several occasions, and it was truly touching to see him kneel down in his silks and satins alongside the cot of a poor dying 'coolie' and engage in prayer.

The Tan Tock Seng Pauper's Hospital in the early 20th century

A Moonlight Band

From Singapore Jottings *by D.I.N., 1885*

It is a lovely Saturday evening, and most of the little world of Singapore are at the Botanical Gardens. The scene is very gay. In the middle of the circular "stand," the Military Band are playing the "See-Saw Waltz." Around, the carriages of the visitors are drawn up in an irregular crowd; some have been deserted by their owners, who prefer walking about in the moonlight to lounging on cushions. A little apart from the band sit groups of young men and women watching the different couples promenading round the musicians...Seated on one of the garden seats at a convenient distance from the "madding crowd," we see a young lady and gentleman who are enjoying the music and the moonlight, and, last but by no means least, each other's company. On the strength of this they declare to each other that they hate Singapore. They hate the climate. They hate the people. In England they were accustomed to have every luxury—except that of pronouncing the aspirate properly... In an open carriage, reclining among soft cushions and wrapped up in a cashmere shawl, a lady—a married lady of course, Singapore is much too refined to allow single ladies to go about by themselves—sits, and by her side, evidently enjoying himself, is a "Military Man." "*Military Man*" again! Lucky dog. Oh that we were military men that the young ladies of Singapore—married of course, we are very "proper" here!—might rush eagerly to "cherish and foster us."

"July 16: At 8 p.m. I went with an Englishman and two Dutch man-of-war officers to the botanical garden to hear the concert by moonlight. It was a splendid night and we enjoyed it immensely until 11 p.m. We then drove to the Hotel de Louvre and heard some music. After every piece the girls come down and sit among the gentlemen, ready to drink any amount of beer, etc. We stayed till 12:30."

From Otto Ziegele's Singapore Diary, *1886*

Waxy-white Splendors

From Sea to Sea *by Rudyard Kipling, 1899*

When one comes to a new station the first thing to do is to call on the inhabitants. This duty I had neglected, preferring to consort with Chinese till the Sabbath, when I learnt that Singapur went to the Botanical Gardens and listened to secular music...All the Englishmen in the island congregated there. The Botanical Gardens would have been lovely at Kew, but here, where one knew that they were the only place of recreation open to the inhabitants, they were not pleasant. All the plants of all the tropics grew there together, and the orchid-house was roofed with thin battens of wood – just enough to keep off the direct rays of the sun. It held waxy-white splendors from Manila, the Philippines, and tropical Africa – plants that were half-slugs, drawing nourishment apparently from their own wooden labels; but there was no difference between the temperature of the orchid-house and the open air; both were heavy, dank, and steaming. I would have given a month's pay – but I have no month's pay – for a clear breath of stifling hot wind from the sands of Sirsa, for the darkness of a Punjab dust-storm, in exchange for the perspiring plants, and the tree-fern that sweated audibly.

"In 1877, twenty-two plants were sent from England to the Botanical Gardens at Singapore. From this small and recent beginning, over two million acres have been planted, and Malaya is now the leading producer of plantation rubber in the world."

William Fitzjames Oldham, Malaysia: Nature's Wonderland, *1907*

Raffles included a botanic garden in his original town plan. It closed in 1829 and another, created in 1836, also failed. The third, established in 1859, became one of the focal points of Singapore's social life and the Straits Government took over administration in 1874.

Holy Mother of the Gods

In the Straits Times, *Apr 1840*

For some days past, the town has been resounding with the clamour of Chinese gongs, and the streets crowded with processions of this noisy race, in honour of a goddess, or the statue of one, that has been recently imported from the Celestial Kingdom, but the procession which took place on Monday was really something worth looking at. It extended nearly the third of a mile, to the usual accompaniment of gongs, and gaudy banners of every colour, form, and dimension. But what particularly engaged the attention of spectators, and was the chief feature of the procession, were the little girls from five to eight years of age, carried aloft in groups on gaily ornamented platforms, and dressed in every variety of Tartar and Chinese costumes…The divinity herself was conveyed in a very elegant canopy chair, or palanquin, of yellow silk and crape, and was surrounded with a body guard of celestials, wearing tunics of the same colour. We have not been able to ascertain the various attributes of the goddess, but it seems she is highly venerated: and a very elegant temple, according to Chinese taste, has been built in the town for her reception. She is called by the Chinese Tien-Seang-Sing-Bok, which, we believe, may be translated Holy Mother of the Gods, being the deity who is commonly termed the Queen of Heaven. She is supposed to be the especial protectress of those who navigate the deep; at least, it is to her shrine that the Chinese sailors pay the most fervent adoration, there being an altar dedicated to her in every junk that goes to sea. The procession, we are informed, is regarded as a formal announcement to the Chinese of her advent in this Settlement, and the exhibition, with the feasting attendant thereon, is stated to cost more than six thousand dollars.

"A trade peculiar to the East is the conveyance of Deck Passengers on ocean voyages and large numbers are conveyed in this manner between Singapore and both India and China, also to neighbouring ports, the larger ships carrying two to three thousand each. Further, Pilgrims to Mecca travel as Deck Passengers and about 12,000 of them embark or disembark at the Board's Wharves annually. When embarking they take with them provisions sufficient for their requirements during the whole journey."
A Short History of the Port of Singapore, 1924

Mustached and Whiskered Sons of Mahomet

The transportation of Muslim pilgrims from the Malay Archipelago to Mecca was a profitable business in old Singapore. In An American Merchant in Europe, *Asia and Australia, 1857, George Francis Train described the Hajjis aboard his steamer.*

Our steamer is crowded with all kinds of men, manners and customs. A party of Arab merchants have attracted the most attention. They are very wealthy, and paid $600 for a small portion of the cabin. Although cabin passengers they keep aloof from Europeans, all huddling round their trunks and merchandise, on which they sleep, eat, and pray, under an awning on deck, disdaining to mix with the infidels at our end of the boat. These singular costumed men of white robe, huge turban, sandal footed, mustached and whiskered sons of Mahomet are bound on a pilgrimage to Mecca, and at certain hours they go off and wash themselves and then come back to pray. It is an unusual spectacle. All arranged in a row, with the chief one step advanced in front, they mutter their prayers kneeling, standing, sitting, now touching their foreheads to the deck, now kissing the hand of the chief, now gesticulating in the most unintelligible manner; again bowing their swarthy forms, again rising; now turning their faces upward and then changing their position, always bending like the forest trees under the westerly winds in the North of England towards the East, or, as they supposed towards Mecca, and, finally, kissing each other's hands at the benediction.

A Coolie a Day

In What I Saw in the Tropics *by Henry C. Pearson, 1904*

As a rule tigers are troublesome only as they steal the Chinamen's pigs, and while there is now and then one who gets to be a man eater, it is not European meat that they seek, but the flesh of the coolies. They are very clever and hide themselves so well that one may almost step on them in going through the jungle. Once they are discovered however, they charge for the intruder, uttering a tremendous roar. If they are not wounded and the charge is avoided, they slip off into the jungle and are almost instantly lost to sight. There is a record of a large tigress with two cubs that terrorized twenty miles of well traveled road, killing on an average a coolie a day for months. She was finally killed by a spring gun, but the cubs escaped. They did not turn out to be man eaters.

"It is well to remark that tiger shooting in Singapore is a very different thing to the sport in India, where the sportsman is up on the back of an elephant or high up in a tree. Here it is a much more dangerous and adventurous matter; on foot, in a jungle, face-to-face at a moment's notice with a tiger. Only bold-spirited men have been successful in Singapore, and there have not been many of them."

C.B. Buckley, 1902

A Tale of Horror

In Trade and Travel in the Far East *by G.F. Davidson, 1846*

Were I to set down the number of unfortunate individuals who have, since 1839, been killed by these lords of the forests, I should scarcely expect to be credited. Let any one look over the newspapers of the Island for the last five or six years, and they will tell him a tale of horror that will make his blood freeze. Many of the more distant gambia-plantations have been deserted by their proprietors in consequence of the ravages of these monsters. Government, in the hope of remedying or mitigating the evil, offered a reward of one hundred dollars for every tiger brought in alive or dead; but so dense are the jungles in which they seek shelter, that their pursuers have hitherto been far from successful. One is brought in now and then, for which the captor receives his reward, and sells the flesh for some forty dollars more; for the reader must know, that the flesh of a tiger is readily purchased and eagerly eaten by the Chinese, under the notion that some of the courage of the animal will be thereby instilled into them.

"It was for a long time a mystery how the first tiger arrived from the mainland, but in 1835 one was discovered choking to death in the fishing-nets off the shore facing the mainland, and in such a position as showed he had been swimming towards Singapore. Since then others have been in the water, all making for Singapore, with the same object in view as the other immigrants—namely, to make a living."

Poultney Bigelow, 1899

The Protector of Chinese

In 1857, a writer accompanying the Earl of Elgin's mission to China and Japan noted that although Singapore "had a population of 70,000 Chinamen," not a single European there could speak Chinese, and ,as a result, Chinese residents were "generally ignorant of the designs of Government". Secret societies filled this vacuum, assuming many of the state's responsibilities, including their members' welfare, the settlement of disputes and enforcement, by secret tribunal, of their own laws. As they carved out spheres of influence, these societies also clashed with the Straits Government and each other.

During a visit to London in 1871, Straits Governor Sir Harry Ord met William Alexander Pickering, recently returned to England after spending almost two decades in China, mostly in Taiwan. Pickering could speak Mandarin, Cantonese and some of the dialects spoken in Fujian, the home of many immigrants to Singapore, so Ord convinced him to join the Straits Government, appointing Pickering Chinese Interpreter to the Supreme Court. When he arrived, he found other interpreters referring to judges as 'demons', police as 'big dogs' and Europeans in general as 'red-haired demons'.

Riots, begun when Chinese immigrants from different provinces took their disputes to the streets, punctuated life in Singapore and in nearby Perak, rival secret societies had since 1861 been fighting a bloody gang war over tin mines around a small town called Larut. Pickering was sent to Perak to lay the groundwork for peace. The resulting Treaty of Pangkor, signed in 1874, brought Perak under the administration of the Straits Settlements and made Pickering a well know Straits figure. In 1877, he was put in charge of the new Chinese Protectorate, an office at which Chinese immigrants could seek Government assistance, and was so successful that the Protectorate became known as "Pik-ki-lin," the Chinese rendering of his name. He was simultaneously made Registrar of Chinese, and in this capacity worked with secret societies to better govern the Chinese population. In 1878, Pickering established the Office for Preservation of Virtue, a refuge for women forced into prostitution.

In 1887, somebody decided Pickering had meddled enough. A hired thug came into his office and, from a few feet away, threw an axe-head at his face. Pickering was hit by the blunt side and lived, but he was so badly shaken that he went into early retirement a year later.

"The Society is called 'Triad' because of the Chinese name often given it, Samp-hap or 'three united,' – Heaven, Earth, and Man; when these three principles are in unison, there is produced a complete circle, or globe, of peace and harmony."
William Pickering, 1878

"When the party was marching up to a stockade and it was not quite certain how they would be received, Mr Pickering would strike up on his pipes. The Chinese would flock out of their strongholds by hundreds and regard the player with wonder, and march along in his wake seemingly delighted with what they doubtless thought was Chinese music."
J.D. Vaughan, 1879

The Chinese Protectorate in the late 19th century

"If the police are the Government's right arm in suppressing crime, then the Protectorate is its very powerful left arm."
Roland St. J. Braddell, Crime. Its Punishment and Prevention, *1921*

Triad Tryouts

From Our Tropical Possessions in Malayan India *by John Cameron, 1865*

Every candidate for admission is led blindfolded to the hall where sit the officers of the society; all the doors are guarded by men dressed in rich silk robes, and armed with swords. A few preliminary questions are put to the candidate, when he is led into the centre of the hall, and the bandage removed from his eyes. He is then forced to worship in silence for half an hour...After this a priest comes up, and opening a large book swears in the candidate: "You have come here uninfluenced by fear, by persuasion, or by love of gain, to become a brother; will you swear before God to reveal nothing that you see and hear this night, and to obey all orders you receive from the society, and to observe its laws?" On the candidate solemnly affirming to this, the laws of the society are read out...

"You shall not reveal the proceedings of the society to any but a brother."

"You shall not cheat or steal from a brother, nor seduce his wife, his daughter, or his sister."

"If you commit murder or robbery you shall be dismissed for ever from the society, and no brother will receive you."

"If a brother commits murder or robbery you shall not inform against him; but you shall not assist him to escape, nor prevent the officers of justice from arresting him."

"If a brother is arrested and condemned, and is innocent, you shall do all you can to effect his escape."

Coolies, Cooks and Crooks

From Singapore Patrol *by Alec Dixon, 1935*

A few busy days at sea taught me to recognize the various types of coolie and to distinguish between workers and drones. It was my habit to feel the palms of men's hands as they filed past the doctor, a trick which never failed to provoke laughter among the passengers. Nine out of ten of the hands I touched were hard and calloused. The tenth – a coolie with the soft hands of a cook – was invariably detained for further examination. This method was open to criticism, but it could be applied quickly – an important consideration when one was obliged to examine over a thousand coolies in the short period of half an hour...Yet it was no easy matter to pick out bandits and professional gunmen by such rule-of-thumb methods, for most of them lived hard, outdoor lives and looked as fit as any coolie or farmer. Political agents, agitators, and teachers were more easily detected, since very few of them were of the muscular coolie type.

Battery Road, late 19th century

An Indispensible Argument

In The Capital of a Little Empire *by John Dill Ross, 1898*

If our Chinese friends do not like a set of postal regulations, or the efforts of the municipality to clear the verandahs, or to keep rikshas in decent order, they close their shops, swarm out into the streets and argue the case with the Government. That is to say they throw bricks and mud at any stray Europeans they find about the street, and if a favourable opportunity presents itself, they bring poles and sticks into play and will belabour any white person who has wandered into their midst with the greatest gusto imaginable. No Chinese polemic with the Government is considered complete without the smashing of a few carriages to enliven its course. A carriage broken up and scattered across the street is an indispensible argument never neglected by a Chinese rioter. It does not particularly matter about the people inside the vehicle at the time, and unless the mob raises the cry of *pah*! they will probably get off with the cuts and contusions inevitable on such occasions. The graceful "gharry" is a variety of carriage much appreciated by the Chinese crowds at odds with the government, because it comes to pieces so easily, whilst the wretched "syce" never fails to give them good sport. During the progress of the verandah riots, I was discussing the turn of events with a wealthy Chinaman, who was evidently delighted at the success with which his countrymen were defying the Government, when one of his servants turned up with the news that the mob had got hold of his brougham and smashed it into splinters. Of course, as I explained to my fat *baba* friend, it was an unfortunate mistake on the part of the crowds, who evidently thought that such a natty turnout must necessarily belong to some European, but he was terribly enraged about the whole affair, and was now for shooting the rioters *en masse*.

"Thirty years ago legalised or semi-legalised prostitution flourished throughout Malaya. Indeed, eighty years ago vice was so rampant that, rather than allow ship's crews on shore, foreign Consuls in Singapore and in other East Indian ports used to arrange for boatloads of inspected prostitutes to be sent on board for the duration of the sailors' stay in port."

John H. Maccallum Scott, Eastern Journey, *1939*

The Lady from Japan

From People in a Native State *by J.H.M. Robson, 1894*

With a rustle, a wobble and a giggle she shuffles by on foot, or reclining in a 'rikisha vouchsafes a passing smile to unregenerate man. Like all the rest of us the little woman comes to the Native States to make money, but unlike us manages to save enough in three or four years to enable her to retire; not that her way of making it would altogether meet with the approval of Exeter Hall, but that is neither here nor there. She is with us and must be accepted as a fact—and a very painted podgy doll-like little fact she is!

The Japanese Government being adverse to the emigration of unmarried women there are often difficulties to be overcome in getting out of the country, but there is money in the business and come they will, no matter what the Japanese authorities do to stop the traffic. Most of them quite understand the situation, though occasionally a Japanese girl will state that she was engaged in Japan to act as a waitress in some Singapore or Penang coffee-shop.

> "The bulk of the Chinese women now in the Colony are purchased in China by bawds and pandas, and have to repay their purchase money and other advances by prostituting their bodies, for years it may be. The lives of slavery and debauchery these poor creatures lead, ending often in disease and death, is something horrible to contemplate."
>
> *J.D. Vaughan, 1879*

Enough Popsy to Satisfy an Army

From Flashman's Lady *by George MacDonald Fraser*

Beyond the shanties was China Town—streets brilliantly-lit with lanterns, gaming houses and casinos roaring away on every corner, side-shows and acrobats—Hindoo fire-walkers, too, my pomaded chum had been right—pimps accosting you every other step, with promises of their sister who was, of course, every bit as voluptuous as Queen Victoria (how our sovereign lady became the carnal yardstick for the entire Orient through most of the last century, I've never been able to figure; possibly they imagined all true Britons lusted after her), and on all sides, enough popsy to satisfy an army—Chinese girls with faces like pale dolls at the windows; tall, graceful Kling tarts from the Coromandel, swaying past and smiling down their long noses; saucy Malay wenches giggling and beckoning from doorways, popping out their boobies for inspection; it was Vanity Fair come true—but it wouldn't do, of course. Poxed to a turn, most of 'em; they were all right for the drunken sailors lounging on the verandahs, who didn't care about being fleeced—and possibly knifed—but I'd have to find better quality than that.

Samsui Women

Samsui women came to Singapore in large numbers. As many as 200,000 are thought to have arrived between 1934 and 1938 alone. From the Sānshŭi District (三水區) of Guangdong, they took a vow to never marry before leaving China, and wore large red headdresses as a symbol and reminder of their vow. Most found menial employment in construction or as domestic servants and were known and respected for refusing to work as prostitutes or opium peddlers.

Home for the Protection on Women and Girls

From A Description of Singapore *by Li Chung Chu, 1887*

Along Kereta Ayer, brothels are as many and as close together as the teeth of a comb. It is said that the licensed prostitutes registered at the Chinese Protectorate number three thousand and several hundred. Apart from these, there are countless unlicensed prostitutes and actresses. They are all Cantonese who were wither sold at a young age and sent to Nanyang or were born and brought up in Singapore...Year after year, little girls from Hong Kong are shipped to Singapore and sold to the brothels in rapid succession.

The Shrine of Iskander Shah

From the Handbook to Singapore *by Rev. G.M. Reith, 1892. The shrine of Iskander Shah – the Malay rendering of Alexander the Great – is believed by some to be the resting place of Parameswara, the Sultan who abandoned Singapura and established Malacca.*

This shrine is on the southern slope of Fort Canning Hill, near the old Cemetery. Crossing part of the old moat by a wooden bridge, the visitor enters the sacred place, and finds himself in a grove of very old and lofty trees, in the centre of which is a stucco-covered tomb, closely railed in. A pan of incense is kept burning at the foot of it day and night; the railing and the trees are covered with the memorials and offerings of the devout. After sunset on Friday and Sunday evenings, crowds of worshippers flock to this place. The shrine is believed to be the resting-place of the Sultan Iskander, one of the heroes of the *Sejârat Malayu*, on what authority it is hard to say. The tomb was discovered by accident after the British settlement in the island, when the jungle on Fort Canning was being cut away. It is a very holy spot for Mahommedans, and visits to it are supposed to cure diseases.

The Nagore Durgha Shrine, seen here in the late 19th century, was built by Indian Muslims in the 1820s.

The Kris

From Tales of the Malayan Coast *by Rounsevelle Wildman, 1899*

I do not know whether my *kris* has ever taken life or not. Had it done so, I do not think the Sultan would have given it to me, for a *kris* becomes almost priceless after its baptism of blood. It is handed down from generation to generation, and its sanguine history becomes a part of the education of the young. Next to his Koran the *kris* is the most sacred thing the Malay possesses. He regards it with an almost superstitious reverence.

The maker of the *kris* is a person of importance among the Malays, and ofttimes he is made by his grateful Rajah a *Dato*, or Lord, for his skill. Like the blades of the sturdy armorers of the Crusades, his blades are considered, as he fashions them from well-hammered and well-tempered Celebes iron, works of art and models for futurity.

The *kris*, too, has its etiquette. It is always worn on the left side stuck into the folds of the *sarong*, or skirt, the national dress of the Malay. During an interview it is considered respectful to conceal it; and its handle is turned with its point close to the body of the wearer, if the wearer be friendly. If, however, there is ill blood existing, and the wearer is angry, the *kris* is exposed, and the point of the handle turned the reverse way.

Amuck, Adverb

From William Marsden's Grammar and Dictionary of the Malay Language, *1812*

العربيـــــه -amuck, engaging furiously in battle; attacking with desperate resolution; rushing, in a state of frenzy, to the commission of indiscriminate murder; running a-muck. It is applied to any animal in a state of vicious rage.

The Dangerous Practice of Amok Running

From Our Tropical Possessions in Malayan Indian *by John Cameron, 1865*

Like other countries inhabited by Malays and Bugis, Singapore is subjected occasionally to the dangerous practice of amok running. In apparent obedience to some sudden impulse, a Malay, or Bugis, will arm himself with two large *krises*, or daggers, one in each hand, and rushing from his house along generally the most crowded street in the neighbourhood stabs at random all who come his way. As many as fifteen persons have been killed or seriously wounded, and many others slightly hurt by one of these amok runners before he was slain, but the killed always bear a small proportion to the wounded and the strokes of the infatuated man fall promiscuously and are ill-directed. As soon as an amok runner makes his appearance, a warning cry is raised and carried on in advance of him all along the street. On hearing this cry a general rush into the houses is made of all the women and children and of all the men who are not armed – no attempt is made to capture the maniac alive, but he becomes a mark for the musket, spear, or kris, of every man who can obtain a favourable opportunity for attack. He ceases to be viewed as human and is hunted down like a wild beast, yet it is surprising how long he will escape death which is aimed at him from every side. Some of these unfortunate wretches have run the gauntlet of nearly a mile of street that was up in arms against them, and have temporarily evaded destruct, some for hours, and others for days. But the end is inevitable, they refuse to be captured, and are ultimately shot down or stabbed.

A Malay village on Singapore's outskirts

"Providence conducted me along a beach, in full view of five miles of shipping,—five solid miles of masts and funnels, — to a place called Raffles Hotel, where the food is as excellent as the rooms are bad."

Rudyard Kipling, From Sea to Sea, *1899*

A Forlorn Traveller

A possible description of Raffles Hotel from The End of the Tether *by Joseph Conrad, 1902*

Scantily furnished, and with a waxed floor, it opened into one of the side-verandas. The straggling building of bricks, as airy as a bird-cage, resounded with the incessant flapping of rattan screens worried by the wind between the white-washed square pillars of the sea-front. The rooms were lofty, a ripple of sunshine flowed over the ceilings; and the periodical invasions of tourists from some passenger steamer in the harbour flitted through the wind-swept dusk of the apartments with the tumult of their unfamiliar voices and impermanent presences, like relays of migratory shades condemned to speed headlong round the earth without leaving a trace. The babble of their irruptions ebbed out as suddenly as it had arisen; the draughty corridors and the long chairs of the verandas knew their sight-seeing hurry or their prostrate repose no more; and Captain Whalley, substantial and dignified, left well-nigh alone in the vast hotel by each light-hearted scurry, felt more and more like a stranded tourist with no aim in view, like a forlorn traveller without a home.

The Raffles Hotel, 1890s

The Hotel de l'Europe soon after it opened in 1905

The Best Hotels in the Orient

From Wanderings in South-Eastern Seas *by Charlotte Cameron, 1924*

A little farther on, facing the water-front, which is ever crowded with ships, is the large establishment known as Raffles Hotel. It has an open ballroom facing the sea, and is profusely decorated with gigantic palms. The entire hotel is surrounded by palms and trees, and here, twice a week, are held dinner-dances and dance-teas. The Europe Hotel has a large lounge with comfortable cane armchairs, always covered in white, and spotless, which creates an effect of coolness, ever welcome in the tropics. The ballroom is in the centre of the dining-room, the dance-dinner nights being Tuesdays and Saturdays. It is generally agreed that there is no choice between the Raffles and the Europe, both are good, first-class, comfortable hotels, and the best you can find in the Orient.

> "Singapore more than any other city is the clearing house for travelers. No matter from or to what ports the traveler comes or goes, from the Mediterranean to the Pacific, he must pass through the Straits upon which Singapore is situated."
>
> *Charles Hendley,* Trifles of Travel, *1924*

A Fable of the Exotic East

The Raffles Hotel is iconic: more famous today, perhaps, than Singapore's eponymous founder. Opened in 1887 by the Sarkies brothers, Armenian hoteliers of Iranian descent, it grew with Singapore through the early part of the 20th century, but was hit hard by the Great Depression which began in 1929. In 1931, the hotel went into receivership and in 1932 its competitor, the Hotel de l'Europe, closed, was knocked down and later replaced by Singapore's Supreme Court.

Raffles was rehabilitated – in 1933 a public company called Raffles Ltd. bought the hotel – and the high teas and dinner dances continued until Japanese occupation in 1942. It was renamed *Syonan Rykonan*, "Light of the South Guest House," and the entrance was moved to face east. The Imperial Army used the building to accommodate senior officers and, when Japan surrendered in 1945, over 300 committed suicide inside the hotel after a farewell *sake* party. Raffles then became a transit camp for prisoners of war transferred from the infamous Changi Jail. By the time the last inmate left, the hotel was ragged and deep in the red.

In 1950, a new manager was hired – Franz Schutzman, a young Dutchman marooned in Singapore while attempting to report on Indonesia's war of independence. Schutzman began to trade on the hotel's mystique. He discovered Somerset Maugham's words, "Raffles in Singapore stands for all the fables of the exotic east," trading permission to use the sentence for a free stay. He sent the recipe for the Singapore Sling, first mixed at Raffles, to the world's finest hotels and opened the Elizabethan Grill in time for the queen's coronation. When King Faisal of Saudi Arabia wanted four large suites and Raffles had none, Franz emptied a floor, tore down walls and welcomed the King the next day.

Franz made diners at the Elizabethan Grill wear dinner jackets and refused to admit an improperly attired Chinese banker, who, out of spite, became the hotel's vengeful chairman of the board. When Maugham announced a second visit to Singapore and Franz again invited him to stay for free, he was overruled. Maugham, said the chairman, had enough money to pay for himself. Franz didn't retract the invitation. He paid the author's expenses himself and, when Maugham left, resigned.

The Funniest Ever Lavatories

Edward Lane, Letters Written to my Children, *1926, describing Raffles Hotel*

This is a very large hotel, and we have practically four rooms – a sitting room, bedroom, dressing room, and a bathroom. The lavatories are the funniest ever – no sewerage connection – but in the bathroom are two tripods with a seat, and of course, the necessary pan and a bottle of disinfecting fluid, and the man calls morning, noon and night.

Raffles Hotel staff

The Nightly Comfort of a Dutch Wife

Hugh Wilkinson describes the Hotel de l'Europe in Sunny Lands and Seas, *1883*

In the hotels about these melting regions, what is called a "Dutch wife" is always provided for one's nightly comfort. Don't be alarmed, it isn't what you are thinking of. My bedfellow and I very soon quarrelled, and, after a short but stormy acquaintance, I remained sole partner of the bed. A "Dutch wife" is an elongated bolster which one places between one's two ankles and one's wrists for as much coolness as is possible; but if mine had been alive she couldn't have been more worrying. She seemed to be most awfully in the way, and as I could get no peace with her in bed, and as she was rapidly getting me out of it, I thought it better to bring matters to a crisis by a tussle and stand-up fight, which was ended in my favour by a vigorous kick, which sent her bang through the mosquito nets to the other side of the room.

ADVERTISEMENTS.

SARKIES BROTHERS,	*Telegrahic Address:*
PROPRIETORS.	Raffles, Singapore.
—o—	Sarkies, Penang.
Raffles Hotel, Singapore.	Sarkies, Rangoon.
Eastern & Oriental Hotel, Penang.	—o—
Sarkies' Hotel, Rangoon.	A.B.C. Code 4th Edition.

RAFFLES HOTEL,
Singapore.

Accommodation for Single and Married Couples.

Cuisine of Highest Character is served at separate tables. Electric bells throughout the buildings.

Visitors and Boarders are allowed to have their lunch at the Raffles Tiffin Rooms, Raffles Square, FREE OF EXTRA CHARGE.

Billiard Room is in a separate block.

EASTERN & ORIENTAL HOTEL, Penang.

The only first class Hotel in the Island.

SARKIES' HOTEL, Rangoon.

The Leading Hotel of Burmah.

Resounding with Merriment and Strife

In Some Glimpses into Life in the Far East *by J.T. Thomson, 1864*

Gambling, to which the Chinese were inordinately addicted, was forbidden by law, but, by the amiable and lax condescension of the governor, it was allowed to be carried on universally over the settlement for a period of fifteen days at the time of Chinese new year. At this period every opium shop had its gambling apparatus exposed to view, and all tribes, Europeans included, dived into the saturnalia. The town resounded with merriment and strife, alternately. The nights were consumed in debauchery, the days in sleep. The vice of gambling was openly encouraged by the opium farmer, and winked at by the Government, as tending to increase returns of the revenue. This fifteen days of excitement redoubled the zest for the forbidden vice. But though forbidden, did it cease? No!

A New Year's Day athletics competition for Chinese residents

"I was much struck by the fact that there were no bedclothes! The Singaporean gets on to, not into, bed; he dons his baju and pyjamas (loose jacket and wide trousers), and lies down to rest."

The Brisbane Courier, *10 Apr, 1875*

Haunts of the Drug that Enslaves

In The Critic in the Orient *by George Hamlin Fitch, 1913*

These haunts of the drug that enslaves were long and narrow rooms, with a central passage and a long, low platform on each side. This platform was made of fine hardwood, and by constant use shone like old mahogany. Ranged along on these platforms wide enough for two men, facing each other and using a common lamp, were scores of opium smokers. As many as fifty men could be accommodated in each of these large establishments. The opium was served as a sticky mass, and each man rolled some of it on a metal pin and cooked it over the lamp. When cooked, the ball of opium was thrust into a small hole in the bamboo opium pipe. Then the smoker, lying on his side, drew the flame of the lamp against this opium and the smoke came up through the bamboo tube of the pipe and was inhaled. One cooking of opium makes never more than three whiffs of the pipe, sometimes only two. The effect on the novice is very exhilarating, but the seasoned smoker is forced to consume more and more of the drug to secure the desired effect. In one of these dens we watched a large Chinese prepare his opium. He took only two whiffs, but the second one was so deep that the smoke made the tears run out of his eyes. His companion was so far under the influence of the drug that his eyes were glazed and he was staring at some vision called up by the powerful narcotic. One old Chinese, seeing our interest in the spectacle, shook his head and said: "Opium very bad for Chinaman; make him poor; make him weak."

High Wages and Unlimited Opium

From Where the Strange Trails Go Down *by E. Alexander Powell, 1921*

In a land where a man has no need for clothing, being, indeed, more comfortable without it; where he can pick his food from the trees or catch it with small effort in the sea; and where bamboos and *nipa* are all the materials required for a perfectly satisfactory dwelling, there is no incentive for work. It being impossible, therefore, to depend on native labor, the company has been forced to import large numbers of coolies from China. These coolies, whom the labor agents attract with promises of high wages, a delightful climate, unlimited opium, and other things dear to the Chinese heart, are employed under an indenture system, the duration of their contracts being limited by law to three hundred days. That sounds, on the face of it, like a safeguard against peonage...Here is the way it works in practise. Shortly after the laborer reaches the plantation where he is to be employed he is given an advance on his pay...which he is encouraged to dissipate in the opium dens and gambling houses maintained on the plantation... This pernicious system of advances has the effect, as it is intended to have, of chaining the laborer to the plantation by debt...Upon the expiration of his three-hundred-day contract, the laborer almost invariably owes his employer a debt which he is quite unable to pay. As he cannot obtain employment elsewhere in the colony under these conditions, he is faced with the alternative of being shipped back to China a pauper or of signing another contract.

Revenue	Expenditure	Opium	Revenue	%
1918	$23, 262, 015	$15, 966, 145	$15, 706, 741	60
1919	34, 108, 465	34, 901, 233	17, 511, 299	51
1920	42, 469, 620	39, 260, 318	19, 983, 054	47
1921	39, 545, 735	35, 430, 899	15, 236, 538	38

Ellen N La Motte, The Ethics of Opium, *1924*

Where the Revenue Comes From

From An American Merchant in Europe, Asia and Australia *by George Francis Train, 1855*

Sir Stamford Raffles showed his good judgment and good sense in making Singapore a free port; for here you have free trade in reality; no taxes on shipping, no pilotage, no import and export tariff, nothing but a trifling charge as light dues. I was at a loss to see where the revenue came from; but when I remember that the celebrated opium farmer pays $15,000 a month, or $180,000 a year, for the privilege of retailing this intoxicating drug to the natives, we see whence a part of it is derived...so extensively is opium used by all the natives who can get a few cents to purchase it.

The Sea Gypsies

From The Hikayat Abdullah *by Abdullah bin Abdul Kadir, 1849*

The Sea Gypsies in their boats behave like wild animals. Whenever they saw a crowd of people coming, if there was time they made off quickly in their boats: if there was not time they leapt into the sea and swam under water like fish, disappearing from view for about half an hour before coming to the surface as much as a thousand yards away from the place where they entered the water. Both men and women behaved like this. As for the children words fail me. Whenever they saw anybody they would scream as though death was upon them, like someone who catches sight of a tiger. All these people brought fish for the Temenggong to eat. None of them knew any way of catching fish except by spearing them.

Boat Quay, late 19th century

People of the Sea

In Trade and Travel in the Far East *by G.F. Davidson, 1846*

Those Malay families whose young men are thus employed as sampan men, are called Orang-Laut, or "People of the sea," from their living entirely afloat. The middle of the river just opposite the town of Singapore, is crowded with boats about twenty feet long by five wide, in which these poor people are born, live, and die. They are wretched abodes, but are preferred, from long custom I fancy, by their inhabitants, who, if they chose, could find room on shore to build huts that would cost less than these marine dwellings.

The Piratical Proa

From The Pirate's Own Book *by Charles Elms, 1837*

The Malay piratical proas are from six to eight tons burden, and run from six to eight fathoms in length. They carry from one to two small guns, with commonly four swivels or rantakas to each side, and a crew of from twenty to thirty men. When they engage, they put up a strong bulwark of thick plank; the Illanoon proas are much larger and more formidable, and commonly carry from four to six guns, and a proportionable number of swivels, and have not unfrequently a double bulwark covered with buffalo hides; their crews consist of from forty to eighty men. Both, of course, are provided with spears, krisses, and as many fire arms as they can procure. Their modes of attack are cautious and cowardly, for plunder and not fame is their object. They lie concealed under the land, until they find a fit object and opportunity. The time chosen is when a vessel runs aground, or is becalmed, in the interval between the land and sea breezes…when the crew are exhausted with the defence, or have expended their ammunition, the pirates take this opportunity of boarding in a mass.

Freebooters in Song

In Horace St John's Indian Archipelago, *1853*

While at their labour, the rowers sing, and play on timbrels of brass, which operate, with a pleasing power, what no promise of reward or threat of punishment could enforce; and thus with song and oar the pirate galley moves under the hands of its crew who, led by one melodious voice, tune their strokes to the sound and find their toil relieved. Thus these hordes of freebooters travel through their Archipelago, conspiring, amid the sunny and tranquil waves, enterprises of murder and desolation against the inhabitants of the coasts around.

The White Raja

From Flashman's Lady *by George MacDonald Fraser*

Who's J.B.? You don't know? Why, he's the greatest man in the East, that's all! You're not serious—bless me, how long have you been in Singapore?... J.B.—His Royal Highness James Brooke—is the King of Sarawak, that's who he is. I thought the whole world had heard of the White Raja! Why, he's the biggest thing in these parts since Raffles—bigger, even. He's the law, the prophet, the Grand Panjandrum, the *tuan besar*—the whole kitboodle! He's the scourge of every pirate and brigand on the Borneo coast—the best fighting seaman since Nelson, for my money—he tamed Sarawak, which was the toughest nest of rebels and head-hunters this side of Papua, he's its protector, its ruler, and to the natives, its saint! Why, they worship him down yonder—and more power to 'em, for he's the truest friend, the fairest judge, and the noblest, whitest man in the whole world! *That's* who J.B. is.

Henry Keppel's Harbour

W.H.M. Read, Play and Politics: Recollections of Malaya, *1901*

It was whilst the *Meander* was refitting at Singapore, in 1848, that Keppel reported to the Admiralty the fitness of the New Harbour for a naval coaling station; but my Lords disdained the advice, and the Peninsular and Oriental Company became possessors of this most suitable site. Subsequently, in 1857, he, as Commodore, commanding the *Raleigh,* sailed that vessel in this haven from the westward, a feat no sailing ship had hitherto attempted. It is not, therefore, surprising that, lately, the name of this harbour has been changed from "New" to "Keppel."

HMS Dido attacking a Malay village

Pirate Hunters

Singapore attracted pirates as well as commerce away from the older trading ports of the Malay Peninsula and frequent, often brutal attacks led the settlement's merchants to petition the East India Company for protection in 1835. A year later, the *HMS Wolf* dropped its anchor in Singapore's harbour, followed by another British warship, the *HMS Andromache*, then another. In just over a decade, the battle for "the suppression of piracy" had been largely won. The men that fought were figures of romance, sailing into unchartered water to fight savage hordes with no advantage but strong ships and British pluck. Foremost among them were Henry Keppel and James Brooke.

The men sailed together in the 1840s, when Keppel was captain of the *HMS Dido*. Brooke had his own ship, *The Royalist*, bought in 1833 with a large inheritance. Both took an uncomplicated view of piracy: Malays at sea and on land were, more often than not, pirates or potential pirates, and deserved to be taught a severe lesson. The men sunk trade ships and shelled villages as well as legitimate targets, eliminating, in their course, many possible sources of opposition to European influence in the region. Brooke used the threat of military force to extract a personal fiefdom from the Sultan of Brunei in 1841, becoming the fabled White Rajah of Sarawak. In 1853, an official enquiry was made into their conduct, but both men were exonerated. Keppel went on to become Admiral of the Fleet.

> "Amongst the Malays, piracy is a national feeling, it is a part of their code of honour, encouraged by their education and habits, and too often fostered by impunity."
>
> *Sir James Brooke,* The Rajah of Sarawak, *1853*

Amuck Against a Host of Enemies

The story of Jaddi the Pirate from The Indian Antiquary, *1920*

Our cruise had been so far successful, and we feasted away—fighting cocks, smoking opium and eating white rice. At last our scouts told us that a junk was in sight. She came, a lofty sided one of Fokien. We knew these Amoy men would fight like tiger-cats for their sugar and silks; and as the breeze was fresh, we only kept her in sight by keeping close inshore and following her…Towards night we made sail and closed upon the junk, and at daylight it fell a stark calm, and we went at our prize like sharks. All our fighting men put on their war-dresses; the Illanoons danced their war-dance, and all our gongs sounded as we opened out to attack her on different sides. But those Amoy men are pigs! They burnt joss-paper; sounded their gongs, and received us with such showers of stones, hot-water, long pikes, and one or two well-directed shots that we hauled off to try the effect of our guns, sorry though we were to do it, for it was sure to bring the Dutchmen upon us.

Bang! bang! we fired at them, and they at us; three hours did we persevere, and whenever we tried to board, the Chinese beat us back every time, for her side was as smooth and as high as a wall, with galleries overhanging. We had several men killed and hurt; a council was called; a certain charm was performed by one of our holy men, a famous chief, and twenty of our best men devoted themselves to effecting a landing on the junk's deck, when our look-out prahus made the signal that the Dutchmen were coming; and sure enough some Dutch gun-boats came sweeping round a headland. In a moment we were round and pulling like demons for the shores of Biliton, the gun-boats in chase of us, and the Chinese howling

A Malay boatman

with delight. The sea-breeze freshened and brought up a schooner-rigged boat very fast. We had been at work twenty-four hours and were heartily tired; our slaves could work no longer, so we prepared for the Hollanders; they were afraid to close upon us and commenced firing at a distance. This was just what we wanted; we had guns as well as they, and by keeping up the fight until dark, we felt sure of escape. The Dutchmen, however, knew this too, and kept closing gradually upon us; and when they saw our prahus bailing out water and blood, they knew we were suffering and cheered like devils. We were desperate; surrender to Dutchmen we never would; we closed together for mutual support, and determined at last, if all hope of escape ceased, to run our prahus ashore, burn them, and lie hid in the jungle until a future day. But a brave chief with his shattered prahu saved us; he proposed to let the Dutchmen board her, creese all that did so, and then trust to Allah for his escape.

It was done immediately; we all pulled a short distance away and left the brave chief's prahu like a wreck abandoned. How the Dutchmen yelled and fired into her! The slaves and cowards jumped out of the prahu, but our braves kept quiet; at last, as we expected, one gun-boat clashed alongside of their prize and boarded her in a crowd. Then was the time to see how the Malay man could fight; the creese was worth twenty swords, and the Dutchmen went down like sheep. We fired to cover our countrymen, who, as soon as their work was done, jumped overboard and swam to us; but the brave Datoo, with many more died as brave Malays should do, running a-muck against a host of enemies.

Gallant and Jealous Men

In Our Tropical Possessions in Malayan India *by John Cameron, 1865*

The men are far more gallant than the natives of other parts of the East, and those they love, they also respect. But as a consequence of the slight nature of the legal bonds that bind man and wife together, and of the ease with which divorce can be obtained by either party, they are jealous in proportion to the intensity of their love. The Malay who knows that a few dollars to the *katib*, or priest, will obtain for his wife a divorce which is valid both in the eyes of his own society and in English law, watches with natural uneasiness the attentions paid to her by another man; and very many of the amoks which have taken place in Singapore have had their origin in jealousy.

An Exceedingly Genial Potentate

Henry Norman, The Peoples and Politics of the Far East, *1904*

The Sultan is a familiar figure in certain circles in London, and he is well known to the inhabitants of Singapore as an exceedingly genial and hospitable potentate, who is always ready to entertain a distinguished visitor, or lend the use of his territory for a horse-raffle or other mild form of dissipation not sanctioned by the laws of the Colony…The Sultan… has rendered great services to the Straits Government as go-between in many negotiations with other Malay rulers, although the latter do not regard him as an equal, on account of his far from royal birth.

A Malay woman with children

The Temenggong Dynasty

Sultan Abu Bakar, "the father of modern Johor", did not inherit his title. His grandfather, Temenggong Abdul Rahman, helped Raffles acquire Singapore, but his father, Daeng Ibrahim, was stripped of his title along with his allowance in 1825. By most accounts, he earned his living as a pirate, until the British deemed him useful a decade later.

In the mid-1830s, piracy plagued Singapore. The Straits Government could not afford to suppress it alone, and the merchants refused to help. In 1841, Gov. George Bonham struck a deal to restore Daeng Ibrahim's title, if he reigned in his followers and helped control Malay leaders. The reappointed Temenggong used his power, and his experience as a pirate, to get rich, monopolising the trade in *gutta-percha*, a rubber-like substance native to Johor. Abu Bakar, his eldest son, was sent to a missionary school, where he learnt English and the manners of a British gentleman. By the age of 18, he began negotiating on his father's behalf and, in 1855, he convinced Sultan Ali of Johor to transfer sovereignty to the Temenggong.

Abu Bakar succeeded his father six years later. He encouraged Chinese immigration to Johor, reformed the government, built an English school and modern infrastructure. He also forged a strong relationship with Britain's royals, enabling Johor to become the only Malay state without a British Resident until 1914. In 1868, after visiting England, he changed his title to Maharaja of Johor, and in 1885, desiring greater legitimacy, he was granted the title of Sultan of Johor by the British.

> "This young man is...idle and completely illiterate; indeed, except by his clothes and consequent personal appearance, not a remove higher on the scale of Civilisation than the meaner of his followers"
>
> *Governor George Bonham's 1835 description of Daeng Ibrahim, Sultan Abu Bakar's father*

Queen Victoria's Memorial Service

From Indiscreet Memories *by Edwin Brown, 1934*

On Saturday, February 4th, the Memorial Service for the great Sovereign was held in St. Andrew's Cathedral. The time had been postponed until 6.15 p.m. to coincide with the time of the funeral at Windsor, and I suppose that never before had such an awe-inspiring service been held there...It had been a dull, sunless day, making everyone conscious of the deep sense of awe and depression that was holding the Empire in bondage at the time, and the attendance at the service overflowed the Cathedral, filled the porches and a large portion of the roads round the building...I shall never forget the reverence and the solemn attitude of that crowd, many of whom, from their position, could see nothing at all, and hear very little but the singing of the hymns.

St. Andrew's Cathedral and the statue of Stamford Raffles in Padang around 1909. In 1919 the statue was moved to in front of Victoria Theatre to celebrate Singapore's centenary.

"The punkah is a sort of long fan hung above the tables, and swung by a servant, which is much used in the East."

Delight Sweetser, 1898

Tiffin

In The Brisbane Courier, *10 Apr 1875*

In Singapore tiffin does not materially differ from lunch in Australia, except that the punkah, the bowl of ice, and the dish of fruit play important parts. Claret appears to be the drink most in favour, though many prefer iced water. Beer is considered too heavy.

There are very few European servants here, and they all have their own peons to wait on them, and carry an umbrella over them when they drive the carriage or go for a walk on their own account. Even the private soldier in Singapore has a punkah pulled over his bed at night. It is quite a sight to meet all the coolies leaving barracks 5 a.m., when they have done punkah-pulling.

Annie Brassey, 1881

Bigoted Punkah Wallahs

In The Golden Chersonese and the Way Thither *by Isabella Bird, 1883*

Yesterday I attended morning service in St. Andrew's, a fine colonial cathedral, prettily situated on a broad grass lawn among clumps of trees near the sea. There is some stained glass in the apse, but in the other windows, including those in the clerestory, Venetian shutters take the place of glass, as in all the European houses. There are thirty-two punkahs, and the Indians who worked them, anyone of whom might have been the model of the Mercury of the Naples Museum, sat or squatted outside the church. The service was simple and the music very good, but in the Te Deum, just as the verse "Thou art the King of Glory, O Christ," I caught sight of the bronze faces of these "punkah-wallahs," mostly bigoted Mussulmen, and was overwhelmed by the realization of the small progress which Christianity has made upon the earth in nineteen centuries.

Moderate Indulgence

From John Cameron's Our Tropical Possessions in Malayan India, *1865*

The universal breakfast hour is nine o'clock, and when the bell then rings the whole household assemble, and should there be ladies of the number this is the first time of their appearance. Singapore breakfasts, though tolerably substantial and provided with a goodly array of dishes, are rarely dwelt over long, half an hour, being about the time devoted to them. A little fish, some curry and rice, and perhaps a couple of eggs, washed down with a tumbler or so of good claret, does not take long to get through and yet forms a very fair foundation on which to begin the labours of the day.

Tiffin time does not bring the luxurious abandonment of the table which it does in Java; people in Singapore are more moderate in their indulgence, yet some show of a meal is in most cases made; a plate of curry and rice and some fruit or it may be a simple biscuit with a glass of beer or claret. Half an hour's relaxation too is generally indulged in, and as the daily newspaper comes out about this hour, there is a goodly flocking either to the exchange or the public godowns in the square for a perusal of it.

The every-day dinner of Singapore, were it not for the waving punkahs, the white jackets of the gentlemen, and the gauzy dresses of the ladies, the motley array of native servants, each standing behind his master's or mistress's chair, and the goodly display of argand lamps, might not unreasonably be mistaken for some more special occasion at home. Soup and fish generally both precede the substantials, which are of solid nature, consisting of roast beef or mutton, turkey or capon, supplemented by side-dishes of tongue, fowl, cutlets, or such like, together with an abundant supply of vegetables, including potatoes, nearly equal to the English ones grown in China or India, and also cabbages from Java. The substantials are invariably followed by curry and rice which forms a characteristic feature of the tables of Singapore, and though Madras and Calcutta have been long famed for the quality of their curries, I nevertheless think that those of the Straits exceed any of them in excellence.

"This equatorial heat is neither as exhausting or depressing as the damp summer heat of Japan, though one does long 'to take off one's flesh and sit in one's bones.'"

Isabella Bird, 1883

Rickshaws in Relay

From Musings of J.S.M.R. Mostly Malayan *by J.S.M. Rennie, 1933*

There were no motors, trams, busses, or trains, and a journey to Serangoon for croc shooting or to Johore for a flutter at the gambling farm, was done by rickshaws in relay, the fare being 3 cents a half-mile. If you want to hear something spicy about your forebears, give a rickshaw coolie 3 cents for a half-mile now, and he will astonish you with details of your ancestry if you understand the Chinese language.

Chinese criers at the racecourse

Hard Lines

From Singapore Jottings *by D.I.N., 1885*

It was a poor old Chinaman
That dragged a rickshaw mean,
He was not great, he was not wise,
Nor very very clean,
But he was honester by far
Than many men I've seen.

And Oh! it was a soldier bold,
Who cursed the waning light,
And did beseech he might be blowed
Particularly tight
If that poor rickshaw man refused
To take him home that night.

The rickshaw man did do his best,
He limped, he hopped, he ran,
The soldier angrily did curse
That poor old Chinaman;
"When will I reach Tanglin like this
You d-------d old Chinaman?"

At last they reach the barracks far,
The Chinaman is glad,
But lo! the soldier gives no fare,
But swears at him like mad.
In fear the rickshaw man retreats,
His heart is very sad.

O! Intellectual Gentlemen,
Please tell me if you can,
To drag a rickshaw or to steal
Which is the wisest plan?

"A rickshaw puller can earn one dollar a day on average. After paying forty cents for hiring the rickshaw, there is still sixty cents left. Unfortunately among ten rickshaw pullers there are hardly one or two who are not opium addicts. It is a great pity that they toil so hard under the blazing sun merely to earn a little money, and yet this little money is entirely consumed by the *chandu*."

Li Chung Chu, 1887

A Rickshaw Strike

In Indiscreet Memories *by Edwin Brown, 1934,*

On October 21st of this year there occurred a rickshaw strike; in point of fact, the last one that was ever seriously to upset the tenor of Singapore's transport problem, and it is, therefore, of more than ordinary interest, and worthy of being recounted in some detail...The strike was well arranged, and was complete. With the exception of a few private rickhaws, there were none out on the streets at all. Residents in these days can hardly understand what this meant to the inhabitant of thirty years ago. I suppose that 75 per cent of the Europeans used rickshaws then to get back and forth to office, and, for the Eurasians and other portions of the populace they were almost the only means of transport.

> "The slums of Singapore were world famous and in the midst of all this poverty and filth, the British lived in oblivious splendor."
> *Tatsuki Fuji,* Singapore Assignment, *1943*

Transporting the Singapore's Diverse Public

From The Critic in the Orient *by George Hamlin Fitch, 1913*

The favorite rig is still the Victoria drawn by high-stepping horses, with coachman and postilion, but the automobile is evidently making rapid strides in popular favor, despite the fact that the heavy, humid air makes the odor of gasoline cling to the roadway. A high-class Arab, with his keen, intellectual face, rides by with a bright Malay driving the machine. Then comes a fat and prosperous-looking Parsee in his carriage, followed by a rich Chinese merchant arrayed in spotless white, seated in a motor car, his family about him, and some relative or servant at the wheel. Along moves a rickshaw with an East Indian woman, the sun flashing on the heavy gold rings in her ears, while a carriage follows with a pretty blonde girl with golden hair, seated beside her Chinese ayah, or nurse. A score of young Britons come next in rickshaws, some carrying tennis racquets, and others reading books or the afternoon paper. The rickshaws here, unlike those of Japan or China, carry two people. They are pulled by husky Chinese coolies, who have as remarkable development of the leg muscles as their Japanese brothers, with far better chests. In fact, the average Chinese rickshaw coolie of Singapore is a fine physical type, and he will draw for hours with little show of suffering a rickshaw containing two people. The pony cart of Singapore is another unique institution. It is a four-wheeled cart, seating four people, drawn by a pony no larger than the average Shetland. The driver sits on a little box in front, and at the end of the wagon is a basket in which rests the pony's allowance of green grass for the day. The pony cart is popular with parties of three or four and, as most of Singapore's streets are level, the burden on the animal is not severe.

A Motor-Horn Symphony

In Malayan Symphony *by W Robert Foran, 1935*

Frequently I saw a long row of taxis on a stand, and each driver was entertaining the neighbourhood with his share in a motor-horn symphony. Some sat upright, putting heart and soul into their contribution to the cacophony of sound; others smoked cigarettes and lolled back in their seats, while keeping *their feet* pressed heavily on bulb or button. The noise produced by this amateur jazz-band can best be imagined than described. It must have been a nerve-racking experience for the occupants of adjacent offices, even as it was for those who passed through the street. The constant sounding of a dozen different varieties of motor-horns and buzzers cannot be recommended as a musical entertainment.

C.B. Buckley, author of An Anecdotal History of Old Times in Singapore, *driving the first car in Singapore.*

Freedom and Cockroaches

Rudyard Kipling – homesick for India and in foul spirits generally – describing his journey from Singapore to Hong Kong aboard a P&O liner in From Sea to Sea

Give me freedom and the cockroaches of the British India, where we dined on deck, altered the hours of the meals by plebiscite, and were lords of all we saw. You know the chain-gang regulations of the P. and O.: how you must approach the captain standing on your head with your feet waving reverently; how you must crawl into the presence of the chief steward on your belly and call him Thrice-Puissant Bottle-washer; how you must not smoke abaft the sheep-pens; must not stand in the companion; must put on a clean coat when the ship's library is opened; and crowning injustice, must order your drinks for tiffin and dinner one meal in advance? How can a man full of Pilsener beer reach that keen-set state of quiescence needful for ordering his dinner liquor? This shows ignorance of human nature. The P. and O. want healthy competition. They call their captains commanders and act as though 'twere a favour to allow you to embark.

Singapore Harbour in the early 1900s

The F.M.S. Railways

In Where the Strange Trails Go Down *by E Alexander Powell, 1921*

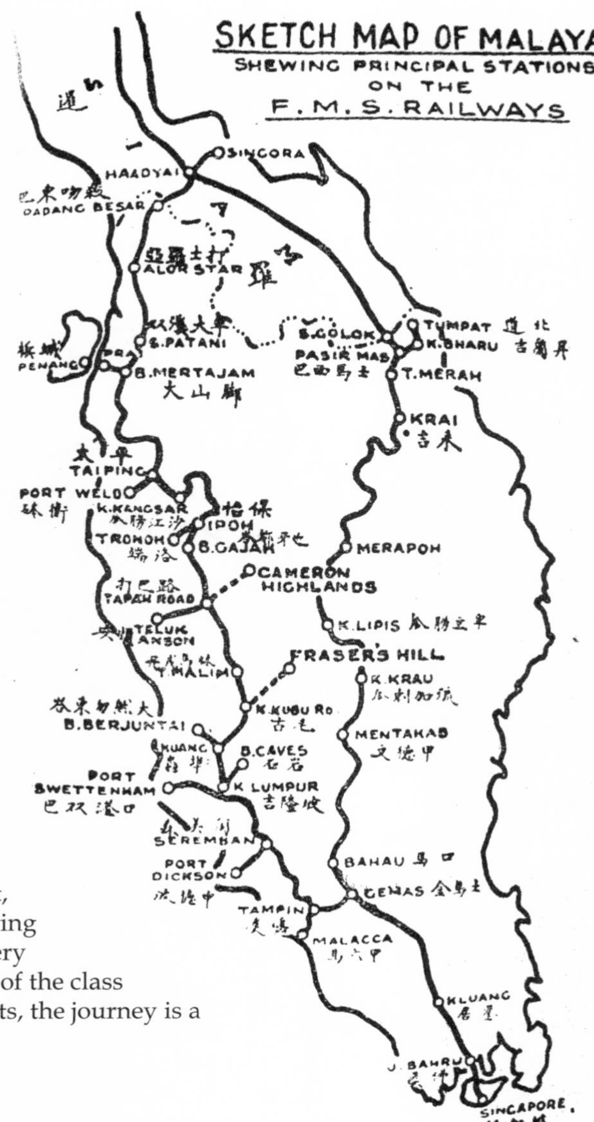

Starting at Johore, which, some Biblical authorities assert, is identical with the Land of Ophir, and running through the heart of British Malaya from south to north, is the Federated Malay States Railway, which has recently been linked up with the Siamese State Railways, thus making it possible to travel by rail from Singapore to Bangkok in about four days. Aside from the heat (in the railway carriages the mercury occasionally climbs to 120), the insects, the dust, and the swarms of sweating natives who pile into every compartment regardless of the class designated on their tickets, the journey is a comfortable one.

Government House

In 1867, the Straits Settlements became a Crown Colony, independent of the East India Company, with its capital at Singapore. Governors at the time lived in a rented house, but Harry Ord, the first to enjoy independence from Calcutta, ordered the construction of a residence soon after arriving. His Government House was constructed in the neo-Palladian style of many of Singapore's other European buildings, according to the plans of J.F.A. McNair. McNair, the colony's Executive Engineer, was also Superintendent of Indian Convicts. He used convict labor extensively: Indian prisoners serving out their sentences in exile made all of the necessary bricks, much of the cement and lime, and had the building and gardens ready by 1869, in time for a visit from Duke of Edinburgh. In 1959, when Singapore gained self-government, Government House was renamed the Istana Negara and became the official residence of Singapore's president.

Government House during its construction by Indian convicts, 1867-69

Shaky Foundations

A description of the first Government House, demolished in 1859 to make way for Fort Canning, from An Anecdotal History of Old Times in Singapore, *1902, by C.B. Buckley*

The Government House is erected on the top of a hill at the back of the town, from which there is a fine prospect of the Straits. As it was completed within a fortnight after the first arrival of the British, it is not to be expected that it can be very substantial. The sides are rough planks and Venetian windows, the roof is attaps. It is withal so unsubstantial that after a Sumatra squall inquiring glances are cast up to discover whether the house is still there or in the valley behind it.

A Chinese barber

> "I was puzzled by the strangeness of the city's skyline when I first saw it from the veranda of my bedroom; yet the explanation was simple: there were no chimney-pots."
>
> *Alec Dixon,* Singapore Patrol, *1935*

A painting of the Padang in 1851 by John Turnbull. G.D. Coleman designed six of the buildings pictured.

George Drumgoole Coleman

Initially a frontier settlement with an uncertain future, Singapore was transformed after 1823 into a city of permanent structures, many of them built to the designs of Irish architect G.D. Coleman. Coleman came to Singapore in 1822. He drew up speculative plans for a Resident's House - which Raffles approved after arriving later that year - but left for Java in 1823. He returned three years later and was commissioned to design two large homes. The second was never occupied by its owner but bought by the government, who made it into a court and later the core of Singapore's Parliament House. Over the next 15 years, Coleman completed important land surveys, planned roads and bridges, designed the Armenian Church of St. Gregory and the first Church of St. Andrew, among others, and helped set up the city's first newspaper, the *Singapore Free Press*. He impressed such an architectural uniformity on European Singapore that his neo-Palladianism would influence many of his contemporaries and the city's later builders, even after the style had fallen out of fashion elsewhere.

The Singapore British

Theodore H. White, Singapore: City and Base, *Mar 17, 1941*

The Singapore British are not as snobbish as the Hong Kong British, more snobbish than the Shanghai British. They are business people, here for 20 or 30 years to turn a profit and enjoy themselves. They play games furiously—tennis, swimming, cricket, rugby, golf. They drink—copiously. When their children reach the age of 7, they send them home to England or, during the war, to Australia to avoid the heat.

The S.C.C. Cricket XI, 1902

"The English are denominated by the Chinese 紅毛 (*âng-mô,* red-haired people); they also dwell in the north-west corner of the ocean, very near to the Dutch, whom they much resemble in person and dress but their language and writing are different. English manufactures are very superior, while their swords and guns, and other implements, are the best in all countries to the north-west."

Ong Tae Hae, A Chinaman Abroad, *1849*

The New World

From Return to Malaya *by R.H. Bruce Lockhart, 1936*

I waved an arm towards the night. With a grin [my rikisha puller] seized the shafts, and off we jogged. Twenty-five years ago we should have pulled up at a brothel, for your rickisha puller, even if he is inarticulate, knows instinctively the tastes of the tourist, and in those days Malay Street was the obvious destination of a European setting out alone at night.

Fashions, however, have changed, and after a gentle trot my puller stopped before a gateway with a huge electric sign in English and flashing the words, "The New World." I got out and rather shyly followed the throng which was streaming through the open gates. Inside was a huge fair with theatres, opera, cinema, dancing-hall, side-shows, booths, refreshment stalls, and even a stadium. The crowd was of all classes and of all races…

The noise was deafening. Next door to an open Chinese theatre with the usual accompaniment of gongs, a Malay operatic company was performing Mashdur. From the sideshows came an endless broadside of chatter and laughter. In the booths in the centre, Japanese and Chinese were selling toys which would have delighted the heart of any European child: voracious-looking dragons, clock-work crocodiles and snakes, miniature baby-carriages, wooden soldiers, and the quaintest of domestic animals.

Avoiding the cinema where alluring posters of Miss Mae West revealed the fact that *I'm No Angel* had been passed by the Singapore Board of Censors, I went into the dancing-hall. There was an excellent orchestra, hired, I think, from some liner. It was playing Aufwiedersehn when I came in, and a crowd of dancers, mostly young Chinese, the men in white European clothes with black patent-leather dancing shoes, the girls in their semi-European dresses slit at the side, filled the dancing-floor. Many of the dancers had their own partners. But when the dance was over I noticed a number of girls who left their partners as soon as the music stopped and went to join other girls in a kind of pen. They were the professional Chinese dancers who can be hired for a few cents a dance.

There were other Europeans dancing, and after asking an attendant how the thing was done I plucked up my courage and, as soon as the music started for the next dance, went over and engaged a partner. More intent on information than on pleasure I ambled slowly round the floor, I had no reason except my own clumsiness to feel self-conscious. My Chinese partner danced with the ethereal lightness of a Viennese. Her name was Tiger Lily, and she told me some of the secrets of her profession.

These Chinese girls are engaged by the management. They are very carefully selected, and breaches of discipline are severely punished. They are paid about eight cents a dance. Each dance is registered on a card, and at the end of the week the cards are vigilantly scrutinized. Girls who are in great request, and who can show a high average of dances, may be promoted. Others, whose engagements are below the fixed average, have their wages reduced. In the dancing-hall, at any rate, there is no social intercourse between guest and professional dancer. At the end of each dance the professional goes back to her barricaded seclusion. The decorum, indeed, was unimpeachable, and could not have been criticized even by a Wee Free minister in a North of Scotland parish. To me this model seemliness was even more extraordinary than the almost complete waiving of the color bar in a British colony.

> "The city has long since ceased to be the wicked city of waterfront dives of the movies. Since the white men's wives arrived after World War I, it has gone respectable. The yellow and brown people (75% Chinese, 12% Malayan, 8% Indian) go to three innocent, well policed amusement parks called the Happy, the New and the Great Worlds. The whites (1.5%) listen on Sunday night to regimental bands playing ancient jazz and folk songs at the Raffles Hotel."
>
> *LIFE, Jul 21, 1941*

More Impressive than Versailles

In The White Man's Rule in Singapore *by Poultney Bigelow, 1899*

At last I reached the Singapore Government House, a palace which stands on a magnificent height overlooking land and sea for many miles. The Governor, a healthy boating and tennis sort of looking man, with honest blue eyes and a soldierly bearing, welcomed me and explained many things. He took me to the top of the roof at the risk of my neck, and made me feel that the White House at Washington could be tucked away into one wing of this palace and still leave lots of room for the Governor. It is a more impressive building than any at Potsdam, or even Versailles. It is vast, yet so beautifully proportioned that the general impression is pleasing.

A Royal Visit

From The Cruise of Her Majesty's Ship "Bacchante" *by the Princes Albert and George (later King George V), 1882*

Government House is outside the town at the top of a hill surrounded with beautiful gardens and park; an imposing building, palatial in style and dimensions. On the second floor is a fine large reception room with a deep marble-floored arcade running for shade along the outside. There are punkahs working the whole length of the immense room, keeping it beautifully cool. The broad staircase leading up to this is decorated with a profusion of flowers and ferns, and everything seems cool and airy. Many of the servants in the house are Chinese; but there are besides Bengalee servants with white tunics and scarlet and gold-laced belts, and with broad, flat, scarlet hats somewhat like a cardinal's.

Appeasing Evil Spirits

Singapore's pious early residents complained that the first Church of St. Andrew looked too much like a town hall. In 1844, a tower and spire were added, but were too heavy for the underlying structure and were twice struck by lightning. The church began to collapse and, by 1852, had been closed, which led to Singapore's first "head scare". Indian convicts spread a rumour that the Europeans were no longer worshipping at St. Andrews because it was occupied by evil spirits. To appease the spirits, the governor was said to require 30 heads, which he had ordered the convicts to obtain by waylaying people at night.

A Crusade against Churches without Steeples

From The Blockade of Quedah *by Captain Sherard Osborn, 1860*

A pretty esplanade, and bungalows standing in pleasant detached patches of ground, stretched away until lost in the jungle and half-cleared country beyond; these, with a very commodious church, constituted the west-end of Singapore: those who built the church, built it to give sitting-room to those who attended; heathens that they were, they forgot the steeple! The good bishop of Calcutta could not—like the Chinese emperor with his old shoe—throw a steeple at their heads; but he did more: he preached a crusade against churches without steeples, and laboured, preached, and subscribed to have steeples put to all Protestant churches so successfully, that steeples went up in the air wherever he had trodden; and I dare say by this time people in Singapore when they build churches build steeples, as they do in modern England, for birds to build in, instead of aisles in which Christians may pray.

The Prince of Pirates

In The Pirate's Own Book *by Charles Elms, 1837*

Among the most desperate and successful pirates of the present day, Raga is most distinguished. He is dreaded by people of all denominations, and universally known as the "prince of pirates." For more than seventeen years this man has carried on a system of piracy to an extent never before known; his expeditions and enterprises would fill a large volume. They have invariably been marked with singular cunning and intelligence, barbarity, and reckless inattention to the shedding of human blood. He has emissaries every where, and has intelligence of the best description. It was about the year 1813 Raga commenced operations on a large scale. In that year he cut off three English vessels, killing the captains with his own hands. So extensive were his depredations about that time that a proclamation was issued from Batavia, declaring the east coast of Borneo to be under strict blockade. Two British sloops of war scoured the coast. One of which, the Elk, Capt. Reynolds, was attacked during the night by Raga's own proa, who unfortunately was not on board at the time. This proa which Raga personally commanded, and the loss of which he frequently laments, carried eight guns and was full of his best men.

Malay rajas

Flag-Hoisting Hills

From A Description of Singapore *by Li Chung Chu, 1887*

Whenever a ship enters Singapore, flags are hoisted on Fort Canning Hill and another hill on the western side to inform all merchants of its arrival. By looking at the design of the flags, one will be able to know what country the ship belongs to, what kind of business it is engaged in, what type of ship it is classified to be, and which country it comes from. These two hills are therefore known as flag-hoisting hills…Whenever there is a fire and the report is made through telephone to Fort Canning Hill, the fort on the hill immediately fires a cannon and a rocket. A flag is hoisted if it happens during the day, and lamps hung if at night. The number of cannons and the colour of rocket, flag and lamp imply which area the fire occurs. One will know where it happens by looking at them. The fire brigade will start out immediately after hearing the sound of a cannon. There are stand pipes along the way and it is quite convenient to sprinkle the fire. Therefore no big fire has ever occurred.

TRAVELLERS WOULD BE SATISFIED WITH THEIR JOURNEY IN SINGAPORE
FOR
THEY ARE ALWAYS READY AND SMOKE "NANYANG" OR "BEAR" AND "TA SHEE" CORK-TIPPED CIGARETTES.

NANYANG BROTHERS TOBACCO CO., LTD.

Shuttling In and Out of Slippery Sampans

In The White Man's Rule in Singapore *by Poultney Bigelow, 1899*

Junks were jammed so thickly together that I could readily have crossed the stream by springing from one to the other. There was a most bewildering shuttling in and out of slippery little sampans that dodged the heavier craft with a speed and dexterity recalling the hansom-cab of London. The men worked silently—naked athletes with earnest expressions playing at a game where the stakes were high, and where much appeared to depend upon moving without fouling a competitor. I missed the profanity and other noises usually associated with the bargee of Western civilization. The Oriental is silent in his anger, and equally so in his vengeance. The knife makes less noise than the revolver...Not a white face did I see on the river, not a single white man's boat. It was all Chinese, with here and there a long native Malay canoe skimming along gracefully under the influence of half a dozen paddles.

The Mark of the Irrepressible European

In Among the Dark Mountains *by David Ker, 1907*

Even in the midst of all these Oriental wonders, however, the "irrepressible European" has left his mark. On the wide belt of level green sward that lies between the city and the blue, shining sea three or four well-watched combats at lawn-tennis are being fought out under the eyes of a wondering crowd of Chinamen, who seem as much amazed at this novel feature of the "foreign devils" as were the Afghans of Sibi when I saw it played there… Nearer to the water's edge several tall sinewy figures in white flannel are rushing about like madmen. The best cricketer of the club has just hit a ball with cries of "Run again!" "Another!" "Another yet!" answered by counter-shouts of "Now, then, look sharp!" "Throw it in?" "Don't let them get another!" while a group of slender, black-eyed Madras coolies look on with astonishment, as if inwardly wondering why "Sahibs" should take so much trouble about nothing. Further on, in the midst of a vast inclosed green wide enough for the manoeuvres of a regiment, St. Andrew's Cathedral flaunts in the dazzling sunshine its daring and not wholly unsuccessful parody of the wonderful architecture of Netley Abbey. High upon the hill above it, commanding a seemingly endless panorama of red-tiled roofs, and broad-leaved palm trees, and tall church-spires, and black-hulled steamers lying motionless upon the smooth bright sea, rise the grassy earth-works and low white wall of the citadel named Fort Canning, in memory of the great statesman who piloted India through the whirlwind of 1857.

Divorced from the Actualities of Life

In John H. Maccallum Scott's Eastern Journey, *1939*

It was an idyllic existence, so completely divorced from all the actualities of life that we seemed to float through it as through a dream. Even now, over two years after, it requires only the faintest of hints – the mention of Singapore, the sight of a Malayan stamp on an envelope, or just laughter echoing over the water of a swimming pool – to bring it all back again, and set us longing for something that scarcely seems to belong to this world – the warm clasp of the tropics coupled with the freedom and ease which is the hall-mark of life as it is lived in Singapore.

Tom-fooleries

In An Anecdotal History of Old Times in Singapore *by C.B. Buckley, 1902*

The first public entertainment in Singapore was given in [1840] by Signer Masoni, a violinist; and in June, the Officers of the 29th Madras Native Infantry, who had just come, allowed their band to play once a week on the plain, which is now called the Esplanade. As long as the Native Regiments were stationed here, the band used to play, latterly twice a week; the chains were taken down opposite Coleman Street and the carriages were driven in, and stood in a circle round the bandstand. Theatricals were proposed as an additional amusement, which led to much correspondence in the Chronicle. One writer, who objected to theatrical performances as tom-fooleries which no rational man would waste his time in, proposed that a fives court should be built instead.

"Restaurants are not abundant in Singapore. There are only one or two Cantonese restaurants and European restaurants respectively. Most of the feasts are held in the gardens of private homes with both Chinese food and European food served. Inns are also very few here, far fewer than in Hong Kong, Canton or Shanghai."

Li Chung Chu, A Description of Singapore, *1887*

The Esplanade

"There are no places of public resort or amusement in Singapore, neither is there any society. The merchants, who form by far the largest section of the community, seem to look upon money making as the chief end and object of their lives, and their topics of conversation rarely extend to any other subject than that of nutmegs or the last price current."

A Bengal Civilian, Rambles in Java and the Straits, *1852*

"What will you have to drink?"

From Two Years in the Jungle *by William Temple Hornaday, 1885*

The hotels of Singapore are all bad, and life in them is exceedingly dull. The liquor consumed in them, and the drunken men one sees almost daily, keep the abstemious traveller in a state of perpetual disgust. The extent to which intoxicating liquors of all kinds are drunk in the East Indies is simply appalling. The drinking habit is so universal, that, as a general thing, when you go to call on an acquaintance at his house, or to visit a stranger in company with other friends, the greeting is, "What will you have to drink?"

The ballroom at Raffles Hotel, described as "the finest in the East"

"I fling jus' pore..."

The Singapore Sling is a drink. It's got gin, cherry brandy, the white of an egg and soda in it. It's red, cold and delectable. I have tried this drink and found there's nothing to it. "After drinking Singapore Slings all day," I could say in a testimonial, "I was not slung at all by the Singapore Slings and I fling just pore, and..."

Earl Wilson, 1951

"The day is supposed to commence at 5 o'clock, at which time a heavy gun is fired from Fort Canning, close to the hotel, making a tremendous clatter. Then ensues a ringing of all the church bells in the place, so that it is odd if you are not roused from your sleep."

The Brisbane Courier, *10 Apr 1875*

Leading a Half-expiring Life

From The Golden Chersonese and the Way Thither *by Isabella Bird, 1883*

The merchants, hidden away behind jalousies in their offices, or dashing down the streets in covered buggies, make but a poor show. Their houses are mostly pale, roomy, detached bungalows, almost altogether hidden by the bountiful vegetation of the climate. In these their wives, growing paler every week, lead half-expiring lives, kept alive by the efforts of ubiquitous "punkah-wallahs;" writing for the mail, the one active occupation. At a given hour they emerge, and drive in given directions, specially round the esplanade, where for two hours at a time a double row of handsome and showy equipages moves continuously in opposite directions. The number of carriages and the style of dress of their occupants are surprising, and yet people say that large fortunes are not made now-a-days in Singapore!

The Singapore Club

The Singapore Club

In Around the World through Japan *by Walter Del Mar, 1904*

As far as I could discover, in the Singapore Club a man is considered abstemious if, before lunch, he has a " peg" of, say, whiskey and tonic-water, followed by a stengah (the Malay word for half, usually pronounced stinger) or split drink, succeeded by a suku, or a split divided between two. The same allowance at lunch and a similar quantity before going home is all the liquid refreshment habitually taken, and the members say that this conclusively proves that a man can live comfortably almost on the equator with an extremely small allowance of alcohol. The club has a fine billiard room, and there are many good players among the members.

Through the Scullery Window

In Two Years in the Jungle *by William Temple Hornaday, 1885*

Our steamer, instead of making straight for the town, describes a perfect fish-hook on the chart, leaving Singapore away off to our right and behind us. We enter a little strait which at first we take to be a river, it is so narrow and so completely shut in by green hills and banks of reddish brown shale. But there are large ocean steamers and ships, wharves, dry docks, and coal sheds all along the northern side; so this must be New Harbor…Entering Singapore by way of New Harbor is like getting into a house through the scullery window. One's first impressions of the town are associated with coal-dust, mud, stagnant water, and mean buildings, and I found it required quite an effort to shake them off. The back door entrance is by no means fair to Singapore, for under its baleful influence the traveller is apt to go away (by the next steamer usually) with a low estimate of the city, every way considered.

"Singapore lives on its shipping; it thrives, so to speak, upon the brine of its harbour, but pales before the massy forest. Yet it has its compensations; it looks forth daily upon the ships of the world, and with the steady eye of its fixed prosperity it gazes forever upon the wandering populations of the sea. The bristling sight from the esplanade is indeed one to astonish an inhabitant of the interior, and the hotels of Singapore are eternally crowded with globetrotters killing time with a distracted expression of haste."

Times Special Correspondent,
On the Empire Trail, *1921*

> "The approach to the Harbour of Singapore is one of the most beautiful in the World and probably only Rio de Janeiro, Sydney, and, perhaps, Hongkong, in any way surpass the panorama of views that meets the eye when entering the Port of Singapore."
>
> A Short History of the Port of Singapore, *1924*

A Constant Floating Fair

From The Blockade of Quedah *by Captain Sherard Osborn, 1860*

Before the town, and at the distance of a mile from it, lay numerous huge junks, all glittering with white and red and green and black; their strange eyes staring with all the vacuity of a Chinaman, and apparently wondering how they would ever find their way to China. Within these junks, in comparison with which we looked uncommonly small, were thousands of prahus of every size and form, stretching away into a narrow and shoal harbour which lies to the right of the town. They were traders from every port of the Archipelago; they had held a constant floating fair until very lately, and had disposed of their wares, completed return cargoes, and would likewise shortly depart for their different destinations. A merchant assured us, that as many as 4000 of these vessels had arrived during the past monsoon...Skimming about amongst these vessels of curious forms and still more curious rigs, there were hundreds of boats in whose shape the ingenuity of man seemed to be exhausted in inventing bodies, intended for propulsion through the water, which should differ as much as possible from each other.

The Armenians

From The Races of Man by Charles Pickering, *1863*

My acquaintance with Armenians commenced at Singapore; and from their European costume, their florid complexion, their manners and familiar use of the language, I did not at first suspect them to be other than English. They were engaged in commerce, and some of them had acquired great wealth. The Armenian church gave evidence of a taste for architecture, that seemed hardly to have been acquired through modern Europe; and unexpectedly, in the East Indies, brought to mind Balbec and Palmyra.

"The most distinguished men as to looks are the Armenians. Although few in number, yet they have much influence from their wealth; they are an exceedingly handsome race, dress after the English fashion, and generally speak English or the Portuguese fluently. Some of them, that I had occasion to visit, were extremely courteous, but spoke of the inhabitants of Singapore generally as of a low class."

Charles Wilkes, 1856

Catchick Moses

From An Anecdotal History of Old Times in Singapore *by C.B. Buckley, 1902*

Mr. Catchick Moses was a man of a very kind disposition, and was much respected in Singapore. The natives in former days used often to go to his house in the early mornings for advice, and to settle their differences. He was a good billiard-player, using his left hand, and he had the curious habit of shaving himself with his left hand, while walking up and down the verandah of the house, without a glass. He made his will about seven years before his death, and gave it to his children to read, so that they could ask him about it if they did not understand it, so as to avoid any discussion after his death. During the later years of his life he did not conduct the business, but he used to come down to town and sit in the office, and go back home at four o'clock in a small palanquin which had been built for him by Mr. G. H. Brown some generations before. He was one of the three local residents who alone wore tall black beaver hats.

TIGER
BEER
虎標啤酒
TIGER BEER
MALAYAN BREWERIES Ld
TIGER BRAND
LAGER BEER
TENAGA BERGANDA

The Singapore Mentality

From Malay Jungle War *by Cecil Brown, Jan 12, 1942*

The atrophying malady of dying-without-death, best known as the "Singapore mentality," largely helped to bring the Japanese 125 miles inside Malaya. For civilians this walking death is characterized by an apathy to all affairs except making tin and rubber, money, having stengahs between 5 and 8 p.m., keeping fit, being known as a "good chap" and getting thoroughly "plawstered" on Saturday night. Singapore thus far represents the pinnacle of examples of countries which are unprepared, physically and mentally, for war.

"The British built up a life of superficial leisure in Singapore. While they drew handsome salaries and did no work, the efficient Chinese and Eurasian clerks slaved."

Tatsuki Fuji, Singapore Assignment, *1943*

The Free World's Key Bearing

From "Singapore: Britain's Far Eastern Fortress" in LIFE, *Jul 21, 1941*

Singapore [is] now Britain's most powerful fortress, and from it the U.S. gets nearly all its rubber and tin...The current battle for the world has spotlighted no single place so crucially. So long as Britain holds Singapore, the Indian Ocean is a British lake. Just so long, Britain and the U.S. and their allies hold nearly a world monopoly of rubber and tin and can cut off Japan's supply. If Singapore falls, the Philippines, the Netherlands Indies, Australia, India, China and Africa fall too. Singapore is in fact the key bearing on which revolves the survival of half the free world.

HMS Prince of Wales leaving Singapore's harbour for the last time.

The Australian Imperial Force in Singapore

From Russell Braddon's The Naked Island, *1953*

Turning right, we sped into a less chaotic thoroughfare and were touched (though surprised, since our journey had been so secret) to observe, slung from one side of it to the other, a huge banner bearing the words, "Welcome to the A.I.F." Our driver, a youthful English private, grinned. "What's the joke," we asked. He pointed down the road over which the banner hung. "That's Lavender Street," he told us. Not finding this enigmatic remark either particularly humorous or informative, we dropped the subject. It was a week before we discovered that Lavender Street is one of the world's most notorious streets of brothels. Obviously, our security had been as superb as the reputation which went before us was high!...The Argylls had held undisputed sway in Singapore for many years and delivered an uncompromising note to all Australians, advising them not to encroach on Scottish territory—in other words: "Keep out of Singapore, or else...!" That, of course, was all that was required. On the first available leave day every free Australian on the Island went into the city. There they were met by every available free Argyll, and great and bloody were the battles—until the Provosts arrived, whereupon both sides, furious at this gratuitous display of officious intervention, ceased battle and fell upon the common foe.

The Fall of Fortress Singapore

Despite their WWI alliance, by 1923 Britain considered Japan a serious enough threat to begin the construction of the Singapore Naval Base. Completed in 1939, it had fuel tanks capable of supporting the entire British Navy for 6 months, the largest dry dock and third-largest floating dock in the world, as well as a battery of large guns, including five 15 inch naval guns with a range of up to 40km. It made Singapore a British fortress - Churchill called it the "Gibraltar of the East" - and lent it an air of invincibility.

Although Japan controlled much of China and Vietnam by 1941, nobody was suitably nervous. Singapore had its naval base, but no capital ships until the arrival of the *HMS Prince of Wales* and *Repulse* on Oct 3, 1941. Despite Lt. Gen. Arthur Percival estimating that he needed 582 warplanes for the defense of Malaya, his command had only 158, many obsolete. There was not a single Allied tank anywhere in Malaya. To compensate, Singapore's infantry garrison was enlarged considerably. Percival wanted the 1940 total of 9 battalions increased to 48 until the RAF was at full strength, but got only 32. Even so, the British were not overly concerned, because a war on Japan was not a war against white men.

The quick thumping delivered by yellow men came as a shock. The attack on Malaya began on Dec 8, 1941, a day after America's Pacific fleet - which Britain thought would sail to Singapore's defence - was attacked at Pearl Harbour. Forty-eight hours later, the *Prince of Wales* and *Repulse* were sunk by Japanese bombers. Singapore now had almost no navy, and the RAF and Royal Australian Air Force were learning just how dangerous underestimating Japanese fighters could be. In little

A Bedazzling Phenomenon

In "Singapore: City and Base" by Theodore H. White, Mar 17, 1941

The naval base is a bedazzling phenomenon. It covers an area of 4 miles. No camouflage can hide its towering radio masts, dockyards, drydocks and machine shops. Roads and railroads crisscross it. Bearded British sailors loll about and Asiatic workmen ride to the workshops on bicycles. The workmen and their families live within the confines of the base itself. Native restaurants and quarters are provided for them. Little brown and yellow babies play about within the shadow of British warships and wives hang out their washing to dry in the sun.

more than a month, the Japanese had taken Kuala Lumpur, just 200 miles from Singapore.

British soldiers still thought themselves "equal to ten Japanese." The problem, they said, was that there were "eleven Japanese." They were wrong. Japan's troops were better organised, more experienced and aided by better intelligence. Supported by fast moving light tanks and bicycle infantry, they were startlingly brave, but not more numerous. On Feb 8, when the first Japanese soldiers crossed the Straits of Johor onto Singapore, Lt. Gen. Yamashita had 30,000 men in his command against Percival's 85,000. After a week of intense fighting, the high ground around the city was lost and the Allies' anti-aircraft ammunition was entirely spent. Singapore's population was under constant bombardment. On Feb 15, the first day of the Chinese New Year, Percival sent a delegation to negotiate with Yamashita and, a little after 5pm, surrendered.

Singapore's coastal battery is sometimes incorrectly said to have been built facing the wrong way. In fact, most of the guns were able to fire in any direction, but were armed with only a few high-explosive shells. Singapore's defenders had plenty of armour piercing shells, designed to explode after piercing the hulls of warships. Used against the Japanese land attack, they would too often strike nothing but the ground, exploding to little effect seconds later.

A Japanese postcard depicting the British surrender.

> "The worst disaster and largest capitulation in British history."
> *Winston Churchill on the fall of Singapore, 1950*

Japan's highly mobile bicycle infantry

The Moment of Surrender

From Singapore: The Japanese Version *by Colonel Masanobu Tsuji, 1952*

Like a magic lantern it all flashed before my mind. How would the heart of the nation be when this news came over the radio? It seemed a dream. Only a few moments ago we were engaged in a life-and-death struggle. "Perhaps I am dreaming," I thought. I pinched the flesh of my thigh hard through my trousers. I was certainly awake and in my right senses. It was no dream. From several places in the firing line cheering voices rose in the air. Then, originating in some corner, the Japanese National Anthem, *Kimi Ga Yo*, spread in a wave over the battlefields.

> "My attack on Singapore was a bluff – a bluff that worked. I had 30,000 men and was outnumbered more than three to one. I knew that if I had to fight for long for Singapore, I would be beaten. That is why the surrender had to be at once. I was very frightened all the time that the British would discover our numerical weakness and lack of supplies and force me into disastrous street fighting."
> *Lt. General Tomoyuki Yamashita*

The End of an Era

From "An Era of Empire Ends at Singapore" in LIFE, *Feb 23, 1942*

Men all over the world, white, yellow, black and brown, watched with awe the massive turning of history. With the fall of Singapore an era of empire ended. White men had taken their most catastrophic defeat at the hands of yellow men since the days of Gengis Khan. The Japanese General Yamashita could say with impunity to the British at Singapore: "I advise immediate surrender from the standpoint of chivalry (*Bushido*) to the Japanese Army and Navy, which already have dominated Malaya, annihilated the British Fleet in the Far East and acquired complete control of the Pacific and Indian oceans."...Though the defeat was military, the 15,000 English civilians of Singapore and Penang in a way had to share the blame. Relaxing and bickering in the level heat of the tropics, they had simply ignored danger.

A postcard carried by Japanese troops during WWII. Soldiers were ordered to sketch their faces on the blank space and give the postcards to children as gifts.

"In those days, to say 'Japanese' of the man or of the language would have earned one a slap. The correct style was 'Nippon-jin' of the man and 'Nippon-go' of the language. A daughter of the family, a girl of twelve or thirteen, was learning the Japanese language. 'How do you like Nippon-go?' asked Shinozaki in English. Replied little miss: 'I'd like Nippon-go better if the go were a little quicker.' "

N.I. Low & H.M. Cheng,
This Singapore: Our City of Dreadful Nights, *1950*

"Perhaps the greatest tragedy of all was the scene on that Sunday morning when the Union Jack was pulled down on the flagstaff on Fort Canning in the middle of Singapore, and that great city, which Raffles founded and our own kith and kin built up, came for the first time under the Rising Sun."

Leonard Gammans, 1944

Japanese Occupation

Japan quickly dealt with the 50,000-odd British and Commonwealth soldiers and civilians it captured in the fight for Singapore. Marched to Changi Prison on Feb 17, 1941, most remained there for the course of the war. Conditions were terrible – prisoners were malnourished, abused and plagued by tropical diseases. But for some, it was even worse. POWs at Changi were among those sent to work on the "Death Railway" in Thailand and Burma, from which few would return. In total, about 27% of the Allied POWs in Japanese-controlled territory died.

Things were equally horrific for Singapore's residents. On the afternoon of Feb 17, Japan's secret police, the Kempeitai, instructed all Chinese to report to checkpoints throughout the city. There, they were arbitrarily "screened". Those deemed innocent of collaborating with China or Britain received a precious stamp on a piece of paper, their clothing and sometimes their skin, allowing them to move through the city. Those "guilty" of collaboration were held for a few days and then executed – most often by machine gun on a Singapore beach – victims of the massacre known as "Sook Ching", or purification by extermination. Though it remains unclear how many died – few bodies have been found – estimates range from 6,000 to 50,000.

Banana money, introduced during Japanese occupation. The currency took its name from the banana palms printed on it as well as the effect of inflation on its value.

"In the spirit of chivalry, we have the honour of addressing you to surrender. Your Army founded on the traditional spirit of Great Britain, is defending Singapore which is completely isolated and raising the fame of Great Britain by the utmost exertions and heroic fighting. I disclose my respects from my innermost feelings...Nevertheless the war situation is already determined and in the meantime, the surrender of Singapore is imminent. From now on, resistance is futile and merely increases the danger to the 1,000,000 civilian inhabitants without good reason, exposing them to infliction of pain by fire and sword."

Excerpt from a Japanese leaflet dropped during the Japanese attack

The Phoney Captivity

Russell Braddon, a soldier in the Australian Imperial Force, was captured on the Malayan Peninsula and imprisoned in Kuala Lumpur. He was then transferred to Changi, as he records in The Naked Island, *1952.*

If 1940 France was the phoney-war, 1942 Changi was certainly the phoney-captivity…Changi was phoney not because of the mass of men in it but because of official attitude behind its administration. The Command determined to maintain full military discipline and establishments, regardless of circumstances or psychology…It meant that officers could not freely mix with their friends who were O.R's…It meant that O.R's were compelled to salute officers whom they had seen cowering at the bottom of a slit-trench…It mean that O.R's were compulsorily stripped of clothing…so that these garments might be distributed to officers who—though they did not work—must, it was deemed, at all times be well dressed. It meant that officers, far from waiting until their men ate and then eating the same food themselves, ate—under orders—in a separate mess and usually before the men…Changi had other shocks. The docile acceptance of Tokyo time as the camp standard…The ceremonial parades at which we were handed from N.C.O. to N.C.O. and officer to officer until, hours later, we were dismissed …The drug selling ring which shamelessly traded M. and B. tablets from our own British hospital…the Spivs of Changi—men with courage and no scruples who went outside the wire each night to collect tinned food from old Army dumps…But if these follies and blacker sides of human nature became obvious to us for the first time in Changi, so did other things which were wholly delightful. For one thing, we hardly ever saw the Japanese (and the ideal life is, of course, one in which one *never* sees *any* Japanese). For another, the common man of Changi greeted us with overwhelming warmth…The men of Changi were solid gold right though, as men, on the whole, always are…Meanwhile, Changi's irrepressible energy—the energy of 10,000 Britons cooped up without any contact with the outside world—burst out in a thousand different directions. There were courses on every subject and every language…On my first night back in Changi I could have gone to lectures on ski-ing, contract law, communism or tiger hunting: I could have gone to any one of four plays or two musical shows: I could have heard Dennis East—peace-time violinist under Sir Thomas Beecham—give a recital. As it was, I went down to the Australian Concert Party, sat on the wood-pile and talked with Piddington and his friends about Australian beer and beaches and possible truth of the prevailing rumour (better known in those days as "bore-holes") that all P.O.W's were to be repatriated by the Japanese in exchange for a bag of rice per man.

Bakaro

From This Singapore: Our City of Dreadful Nights *by N.I. Low & H.M. Cheng, 1950. Bakaro means idiot or fool in Japanese.*

The Japanese delegates alighted from their cars at High Street and marched to the Municipal Building, flanked by British Military Police. As they passed, the crowds shouted "Bakaro!" The "Bakaros" of a thousand throats expressed the pent up hatred of the Nip, a hatred generated by the excesses of the Nip at his coming and deepened during the three and a half years of his occupation..."Bakaro" is a word often in the mouths of the irate Nips of our acquaintance, generally going with a buffet or a kick, or both. We had often had it applied to us, and now, at long last, we could safely apply it to the Nip—to Nip generals! ...For days afterwards, whenever a white man appeared in Chinatown, he was sure to be surrounded by Chinese boys, and their obvious pleasure at the sight of him must have embarrassed many a shy man, they tumbling over each other in their eagerness to touch him, hailing him as "Joe" and, irreverent as ever, referring to him among themselves as "Red Haired Devil", but in affection, as it were pronouncing a pet-name caressingly, and he grinning like a veritable jackass, vainly striving to express goodwill and fellow-feeling, neither conversant with the other's lingo.

Hara-kiri in the Reservoirs

From The Glasgow Herald, Nov 7, 1946

Not only did the Japanese neglect the waterworks during their occupation, but quite a number of the more extreme Bushido men made their final protest against capitulation by committing *hara-kiri* in the reservoirs. Some time elapsed before these bodies were discovered. In the interval they did not appreciably affect the flavour of the "compo"ies which the relief force drank before it acquired a taste for saké.

Changi Prison

From King Rat *by James Clavell, 1962*

Changi was set like a pearl on the eastern tip of Singapore Island, iridescent under the bowl of tropical skies. It stood on a slight rise and around it was a belt of green, and farther off the green gave way to the blue-green seas and the seas to infinity of horizon. Closer, Changi lost its beauty and became what it was — an obscene forbidding prison. Cellblocks surrounded by sun-baked courtyards surrounded by towering walls. Inside the walls, inside the cellblocks, story on story, were cells for two thousand prisoners at capacity. Now, in the cells and in the passageways and in every nook and cranny lived some eight thousand men... These men too were criminals. Their crime was vast. They had lost a war. And they had lived.

A sketch of Changi Prison by Ronald Searle, done during his imprisonment there. Searle hid his drawings under the mattresses of prisoners dying of cholera.

The Straits Times

From An American Merchant in Europe, Asia and Australia *by George Francis Train, 1857*

The Straits Times press establishment comprise letter press, copperplate, and lithographic work; bookbinding in all its branches; and has a very extensive job printing business. The workmen consist of Hindoos, Portuguese, Chinese, Malays, Javanese and Klings (natives of the Coromandel coast) and it is most remarkable to see how well they do their work, in a language they do not understand.

"Naturally, like everybody else, I was a diligent reader of the excellent and always interesting *Singapore Free Press*... I keep my regard for that paper to this day. It was certainly the newspaper of the East between Rangoon and Hong Kong."
Joseph Conrad, 1917

Raffles Lighthouse

From A Lady's Second Journey around the World *by Ida Pfeifer, 1855*

In Singapore itself I found nothing altered, but a magnificent lighthouse had been built during that time, about twenty miles off the island, on a rock in the sea, where there is so tremendous a surf that the guardians of the lighthouse are kept furnished with fresh water and provisions for six months. The tower took eighteen months to build, and is constructed of masses of granite brought from the neighbouring island of Urbin.

The Bugis

Bugis, described here by G.F. Davidson in his 1846 Trade and Travel in the Far East, *were among the first people to trade and settle at Singapore. Although a distinct ethnic group, from the island of Sulawesi, the word was also applied to people from Borneo and the rest of what is today Indonesia.*

The native traders next in importance to the Chinese, are the Bugis. These arrive in October and November, bringing in their uncouth-looking vessels, large quantities of coffee of very good quality, gold-dust, tortoise-shell, native clothes (celebrated all over the Archipelago for their durability), béche-de-mer, deer-sinews, rice, &c...They are a troublesome set to deal with, and require the exercise of more patience than a European in these parts generally possesses. They are, however, always received with a hearty welcome by the Chinese of the Island, who, inviting them to be seated, immediately hand round the *siri-box* (betel-nut, arica leaf, &c.) among them; and over this universal luxury, they will sit and talk on business matters for hours, during which time it may be fairly calculated that both host and guests tell a lie per minute, without betraying by their countenances the slightest consciousness of having been thus engaged. This strange sort of preliminary negotiation goes on, probably, for a week; at the end of which the passer-by may see the contents of the different Bugis boats entering the Chinese shops or stores, as the case may be. On getting rid of his import cargo, the Bugis trader takes a few days more to rest and refresh himself, before he begins looking round for a return cargo, which usually consists of opium, iron, steel, cotton yarn, cotton goods, gold thread, &c. He seldom or never takes money away with him... Their crews are not allowed to land armed with the *kriss* or any other weapon; a wise precaution, as they are rather too fond of having recourse to them in the event of any quarrel or misunderstanding with those with whom they deal.

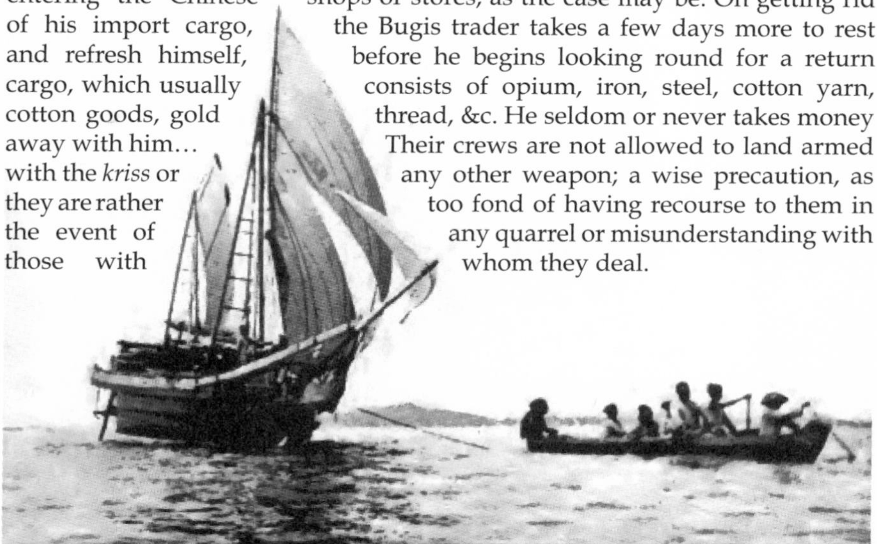

Inside a Hot Cardboard Box

From Present Indicative *by Noel Coward, 1931*

On the first evening I spent in Singapore, I sat on the verandah of the hotel, sipping a gin-sling and staring at the muddy sea. There was a thunderstorm brewing, and the airless heat pressed down on my head. I felt as though I were inside a hot cardboard box which was growing rapidly smaller and smaller, until soon I should have to give up all hope of breathing and die of suffocation.

Toilers from Many Lands

In The Critic in the Orient *by George Hamlin Fitch, 1913*

Hong Kong streets may have seemed to present an unparalleled mixture of races; Canton's narrow alleys may have appeared strange and exotic; but Singapore surpasses Hong Kong in the number and picturesqueness of the races represented in its streets, as it easily surpasses Canton in strange sights and in swarming toilers from many lands that fill the boats on its canals and the narrow, crooked streets that at night glow with light and resound with the clamor of alien tongues.

Malay St., early 1900s

The New Singapore

From Return to Malaya *by R.H. Bruce Lockhart, 1936*

Malay Street itself brought me face to face with the new Singapore. Gone was Madame Blanche with her collection of Hungarians, Poles and Russian Jewesses – the frail army of white women recruited by the professional pimps from the poorest population of Central and Eastern Europe, and drifting farther East as their charms declined, via Bucharest, Athens and Cairo, until they reached the ultima Thule of their profession in Singapore. There had been no English girls among them. On political grounds the British administration has always maintained a ban on the British prostitute...Gone, too, were the long rows of Japanese brothels with their lower windows shuttered with bamboo poles behind which sat the waiting odalisques, discreetly visible, magnificent in elaborate head-dress and brightly coloured kimonos, heavily painted and powdered, essentially doll-like and yet not without a certain charm which in romantic youths like myself inspired a feeling more of pity than desire.

An Amok Stabs the British Resident

In 1823, Syed Yassin, a Muslim trader from Penang and a descendant, he claimed, of Mohammed, ran amok. Yassin owed money to Syed Omar Aljunied, an Arab resident, and was put into prison because he was unable to pay it back. He somehow smuggled a kris into his cell and obtained permission to visit Aljunied at home, to plead, he claimed, for his debts to be forgiven. A single servant, described as a "Hindoo peon", accompanied him. Aljunied luckily saw Yassin arrive, guessed his intentions and fled along the river to Farquhar's house.

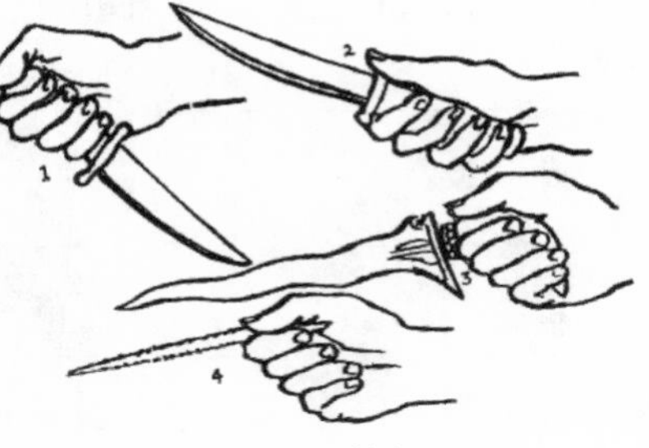

Daggers and krisses

When Aljunied returned, accompanied by Farquhar, his son, five sepoys and their commanding officer, Yassin had killed the peon and vanished. It was almost dark, but Farquhar searched Aljunied's compound; he paused at the veranda, poked his stick through the trees around it and Yassin – who had hidden underneath the veranda – pounced, stabbing the Resident in the chest before he was brought down by Farquhar's son and bayoneted to death.

Farquhar lived, but confusion followed. It was suggested that the attack had been organised by the Temenggong, Singapore's Malay chieftain. Stamford Raffles had been in Singapore since October the previous year, and by the time he arrived at Aljunied's home, the sepoys had their guns trained on the Temenggong's compound. Yassin's body was mutilated beyond recognition and his identity was uncertain; when his motives were established, Raffles ordered the sepoys to stand down and had Yassin's corpse dragged to the centre of town. After Yassin's body had been paraded in a buffalo cart, it was hung in a cage for two weeks. Yassin was then buried at Tanjong Pagar. Strangely, perhaps because he had "only killed a Fakir (the Hindoo) and wounded a Nazarene (Colonel Farquhar)", his grave became a place of pilgrimage.

Race Riots

Singapore's merger with the Federation of Malaysia was awkward. Economic disparities between the sophisticated port city and Malaysia's hinterland were represented by some as evidence of Malay exploitation by Britain and its Chinese puppet, the People's Action Party. Identity politics led, inevitably, to communal violence. On July 21, 1964, during a celebration of the Prophet Mohamed's birthday, a riot broke out near the Kallang Bridge. Malays, provoked by a series of fiery speeches and a long day in the sun, attacked first the police and then Chinese passers-by. A curfew was imposed a few hours later; when it was lifted the next morning, the rioting continued. It was 11 days before the curfew could be lifted again, by which time 23 people had been killed, 450 injured and 3,000 arrested. Little more than a month later, the city was again under lock-down. On Sept. 3, a Malay trishaw-rider was murdered in a Chinese neighbourhood, sparking another riot, which injured another 106 people and left 13 more dead.

A Malay soldier manning a bren gun during the Malayan Emergency

A Lesson in Capitalism

In 1959, Singapore obtained self-government over all internal affairs. In the subsequent election, the People's Action Party won 43 of 51 seats and its leader, Lee Kuan Yew, became the first Prime Minister of Singapore. Although the island's capitalists distrusted the left-leaning party, and some went as far as relocating to Kuala Lumpur, Lee soon proved himself a pragmatist – as a TIME *journalist observed in this report from Nov 7, 1960.*

Taking office, they poured out their avenging anti-Western zeal by ripping down Queen Elizabeth's portrait, slashing British bureaucrats' salaries, banning jukeboxes, comic books and other manifestations of what they called the West's 'yellow culture.' Tieless, coatless puritans presiding over the sybaritic center of the old South Seas, they rapidly got a name as Southeast Asia's most honest administrators...But Prime Minister Lee, a wealthy, Cambridge-schooled Chinese, soon grasped that Singapore by itself is an island emporium ill suited to revolutionary socialism since, among other things, it lacks any major industries to nationalize. His revised economic policy: 'Teaching the capitalists how to run their system.'

A Vessel Independent of the Wind

A description of the 1837 encounter between the first steamer built in India, the Diana, and pirates from An Anecdotal History of Old Times in Singapore *by CB Buckley, 1902*

The pirates in six large prahus, seeing the smoke, thought it was a sailing ship on fire, so they left the Chinese junk which they were attacking, and bore down on the steamer, firing on her as she approached. To their horror, the vessel came close up against the wind, and then suddenly stopped opposite each prahu, and poured in a destructive fire, turning and backing quite against the wind, stretching the pirates in numbers on their decks. A vessel that was independent of the wind was, of course, a miracle to them.

"Singapore is everything we could desire; it breaks the spell; and [the Dutch] are no longer the exclusive sovereigns of the Eastern Seas."

Stamford Raffles, Jun 1819

Singapore

From Rudyard Kipling's The Seven Seas, *1900*

Hail, Mother! East and West must seek my aid
Ere the spent gear shall dare the ports afar.
The second doorway of the wide world's trade
Is mine to loose or bar.

"Singapore harbor commands one of the greatest natural turnstiles of commerce. Shipping has no other option than to use it."
Frederic Courtland Penfield, East of Suez, 1899

Reverend Pierre Paris

A description of Pierre Paris, a La Salle Brother stationed in Singapore, from An Anecdotal History of Old Times in Singapore, *by C.B. Buckley, 1902*

A remarkable character in Singapore was the Rev. Pierre Paris, who was born on 19th January, 1822, at Fontenis, Haute-Saone, and was a peasant boy working in the fields, which was no doubt a good preparation for the work he afterwards did in Singapore, where he spent long hours trudging about in the jungle between the different huts of his congregation. He went into the priesthood, commencing to learn Latin at eighteen years of age, and after being a vicar in a country parish for four years joined the Society of Foreign Missions in 1854. On 27th June, 1855, he left Antwerp for the Straits. After a short time in Penang he went to Malacca, where he learnt the patois spoken by the Portuguese there, and Tamil and Chinese. He was a good linguist, speaking several dialects of Chinese. As an example of the way he used to move about, he might be seen on Sunday morning walking into town along Serangoon Road, for there were no jinrikishas then, with his Chinese umbrella in one hand and a stick in the other. He had said mass and preached in Chinese at Serangoon, and was walking seven miles into town to hold the service in Tamil at eleven o'clock. After that he would hold a service in the jail; at 2 o'clock he had Catechism for the Chinese children, and at 3 o'clock evening service in the Chinese Church of S.S. Peter and Paul. It had been through his exertions that this fine Church had been built in the town in 1871.

St. Joseph's School on Brass Bassah Road

Sent Out into the Jungles

From Reminisces of an Indian Official *by General Sir Orfeur Cavenagh, 1884*

It was arranged that two parties, of eight convicts each, should be furnished with arms and ammunition, and sent out into the jungles, where they would be allowed to remain, merely coming to attend the monthly muster, so long as they succeeded in destroying a tiger every three months, they being at the same time allowed to receive the Government reward as a stimulus to their exertions. The number of tigers soon diminished, and the necessity for the second party ceased.

"An English sailor who had come from Singapore was eaten by ants. He had been to Johore, where a Chinaman had served him with drink. He was probably overcome by the heat, and lay down. The ants had overpowered him in some way, and the next morning he was found dead."

John Fairlie, Life in the Malay Peninsula, *1892*

Large Eating

From Otto Ziegele's Singapore Diary of 1886

Aug. 13: Great Chinese fete this evening, very amusing. They cover a table with all sorts of eatables, to their ideas the best of the best; then they lay knives and forks and pour out some brandy in glasses and put three or four chairs ready, in which their gods are supposed to sit and feed. Next to the chairs they put a basin of water and a towel, for the gods to dry their hands. Just near this they kick up an immense row with all sorts of infernal instruments and sing. Everywhere lanterns and thin smoking sticks, also incense (sandalwood, etc.) is burnt. This is kept up all night and in Malay is called *Makan Besar* (large eating). The whole affair is very absurd, the gods seem to be very fond of liquor as each god has a large bottle of gin and three bottles of whisky or rum in front of him.

A Penal Colony

In 1788, a year after it began sending convicts to Australia for the first time, Britain started sending Indians serving sentences of seven years or more to Bencoolen, the settlement on Sumatra that Raffles would later govern. When Bencoolen became Dutch in 1824, the prisoners were moved to Singapore, which became the British Raj's most important penal colony with a population, by 1857, of 3,000 convicts. They were far from unwelcome: boomtown Singapore had labor shortages, so prisoners were put to work filling marshland, laying roads, constructing government buildings, felling trees, making bricks and even putting out fires or hunting tigers.

The government rewarded hard work with a measure of freedom. Divided into six different classes, according to the severity of their crimes, and given different fetters, different work and even different pay, convicts were otherwise allowed to move freely through town. Good behavior resulted in promotion and the system proved so effective that a class of convict officers, responsible for other inmates, was created. The system was nevertheless stopped in 1860, because of the Sepoy Mutiny in India. Singapore's residents were terrified by the prospect of bitter, war-toughened soldiers, responsible for the deaths of white men in India, arriving on the island, and convicts were from then on sent to the Andaman Islands.

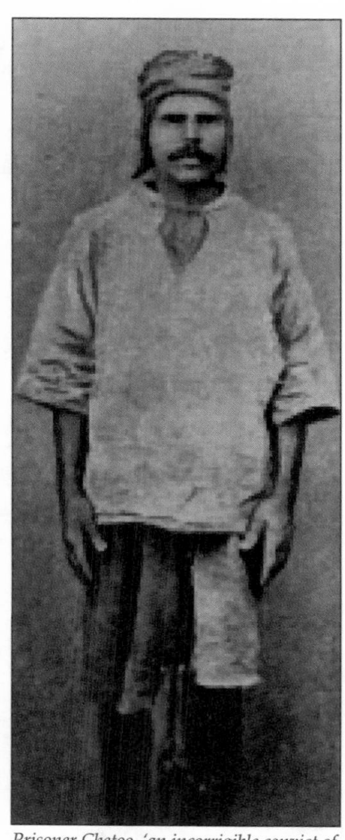

Prisoner Chetoo, 'an incorrigible convict of the fifth class.'

> "Owing to caste prejudices, transportation across the seas was to many of the Indian convicts worse than death itself, for it carried with it not only expulsion from caste, but, owing to their wrong conception of fate, or "nusseeb" as they call it, a dread of pain and anguish in another existence."
>
> *J.F.A. McNair,* Prisoners their own Warders, *1899*

Well Behaved Convicts

From Reminisces of an Indian Official *by General Sir Orfeur Cavenagh, 1884*

Every convict on his arrival was placed in the lowest grade and worked as an ordinary labourer, in irons, for a specified term of years; at the expiration of that period, in the event of his having a sufficiently clear defaulter's-sheet…he was promoted to a higher class, his fetters were lightened, and if he showed an aptitude for learning any handicraft he was transferred to the workshops and taught some trade. When the second term elapsed, he was in like manner again promoted, and employed as an artificer, receiving, according to his merits, some slight remuneration for his services. At the end of the third period he was raised to the position of petty officer, and was permitted to leave the precincts of the jail for a short time after working hours. The full term of probation having expired, he was granted a ticket-of-leave, on condition, however, of providing a suitable security, who became bound for his good behaviour...As a rule the convicts were very well behaved, and shortly after my arrival at Singapore, I was much struck by a remark made by the commissioner of police, who was referring to the case of a lady who had wandered into the jungle and lost her way; and stated that although her husband was much alarmed, as she wore some valuable jewels, the moment he heard that she had fallen in with a party of convicts employed in road-making, he ceased to have any fears for her safety.

A Full Measure of Punishment

In Sir Hugh Charles Clifford's In a Corner of Asia, *1899*

307 looked round him at the strange scene with curious eyes. It was a mixed group of Orientals, Chinese of half-a-dozen tribes, Tamils from Southern India, Malays from many States of the Peninsula and from various islands of the Archipelago, a Muhammadan Bengali or two, and one stray Siamese. They were a peculiarly healthy body of men, very hard and spare, well-fed, well-nurtured, but with hardly a pound of superfluous flesh among them all. This is the merit of our prison system in the East. We feed our convicts sufficiently and well, but they rise from every meal feeling the least little bit hungry, and they work day in and day out with the untiring regularity of machines. Also, they go to bed early and rise when the dawn is still grey. All this makes for health, and the sheer regularity of the thing bores the native more intensely, and wearies the soul out of him more effectually than any white man can easily conceive. The divorce from tobacco and opium, and the complete separation from his women-folk also take away from the native, all, or nearly all the things which represent pleasure to him, and thus, though we have robbed imprisonment of the horrors which were inseparable from confinement in the barbarous gaol-gages of Independent Malaya, the deprivations, the monotony, and, in no small degree, the very cleanliness of the life to which we condemn our Asiatic convicts, carries with it for them a full measure of punishment.

Missionaries

Until the end of the first Opium War in China and the French colonisation of Vietnam, missionaries were unwelcome in much of the Far East. Singapore was an exception: safe and diverse, an ideal place to learn languages and translate bibles, it was where a Thai typeface was first used and Chinese typography expanded to 3,000 characters for the purpose of printing a bible. With missionaries came schools. The oldest girls school in Singapore, St. Margaret's, was opened by Maria Dyer of the London Missionary Society. A La Salle brother, Jean-Marie Beurel, established the St. Joseph's Institution, the island's third oldest school. But Singapore's evangelical usefulness waned when China was forced open. In 1839, the American Board of Commissioners of Foreign Missions moved to Shanghai. The London Missionary Society relocated less than ten years later. Singapore was quickly emptied of missionaries anxious to save China's many more souls, but one man refused to go. Benjamin Keasberry severed his ties with both organisations and ran his own mission, which included a school, printing press and a church - the Malay Chapel on Prince's Street, nicknamed *Greja Keasberry*, or Keasberry's Church - until his death, in the pulpit, in 1875.

St, Joseph's Institution

The Moral Improvement of the Natives

From Travels in South Eastern Asia by Howard Malcolm, 1839

From the first settlement of Singapore by the British, operations for the moral and religious improvement of the natives have been carried out. Translations into Malay, and the printing and distribution of tracts and Scriptures, engrossed most of the time of early missionaries. In this department, a good deal has been done; but, so far as can now be seen, with very little success. Not a single Malay in Singapore has made even a nominal profession of Christianity; nor are there any hopeful catechumens. For a long time past, no one competent in the language has resided here; so that the only missionary efforts are the distribution of tracts, and some unpromising schools.

A Strange Remnant of Ancestral Pride

In Our Tropical Possessions in Malayan India *by John Cameron, 1865*

They are still called the Portuguese, but they have long ago ceased to deserve to be distinguished, at least favourably so, from the native inhabitants. Indeed they have so intermarried with the Malays and other native people that they would now with great difficulty be distinguished from them, if it were not that, with a strange remnant of ancestral pride, they rigidly adhere to the European style of dress. Nor do the minds of these people show any indication of their superior descent; they are not clever or industrious, and not ambitious. It seems that as soon as they accumulate a little money, either by accident or labour, they cease working and either live in indolence until it is spent, or as is more frequently the case—for they are given to good-fellowship among themselves—they have one grand " blow out."

A "Happy" Eurasian Family

From J.T. Thomson's Glimpses into Life in the Far East, *1864*

The head of the family was of mixed race, but educated in Europe. His wife was of pure British blood, but was reared and educated in India. The husband had children before his marriage by native women; his wife had been married before, and had children by both her husbands. All lived together in great amity in the same house. Some of the children were as dark as Hindoos, other were as fair as Swedes; but there was this difference made, and admitted to be correct on all sides, that the fair ones went to evening parties, while the dark ones stayed at home. The fair ones were expected to take a leading part, and so were attentively educated; the dark ones were intended for humbler usage, and so had little spirit in them. Such were the arrangements that a happy Eurasian family fell into, without involving dispute or disagreement.

The Bible House

A Father to His Flock

From The Malay Archipelago *by Alfred Russel Wallace, 1869*

My friend at Bukit-tima was truly a father to his flock. He preached to them in Chinese every Sunday, and had evenings for discussion and conversation on religion during the week. He had a school to teach their children. His house was open to them day and night. If a man came to him and said, "I have no rice for my family to eat to-day," he would give him half of what he had in the house, however little that might be. If another said, "I have no money to pay my debt," he would give him half the contents of his purse, were it his last dollar. So, when he was himself in want, he would send to some of the wealthiest among his flock, and say, "I have no rice in the house," or "I have given away my money, and am in want of such and such articles." The result was that his flock trusted and loved him, for they felt sure he was their true friend, and had no ulterior designs in living among them.

> "One of the missions was planning to build, when they were offered such an unusual and excessive price for their ground that they accepted it. It developed afterwards that a rich Chinaman who had a home nearby discovered that at certain times of the moon the projected building would bring him bad luck; so he paid the price and kept away the evil spirits. The Chinese do not cater to the good spirits, saying that they will take care of themselves."
>
> *Charles Hendley,* Trifles of Travel, *1924*

Church of the Good Shepherd

One of the Greatest Sea Ports

In A Short History of the Port of Singapore, *1924*

5,764 merchant vessels, representing a tonnage of 8,538,853 tons, entered the port of Singapore in the year 1920, and of these vessels, 2,899 were British, 1,324 Dutch and 638 Japanese, the remaining 903 being American, French, Siamese and other nationalities. Singapore is therefore one of the greatest sea-ports in the world and, according to Whitaker 1922, in the matter of tonnage entered and cleared, ranks next below Liverpool.

Victoria Dock in the 1890s

The Real Importance of Singapore

From The Capital of a Little Empire *by John Dill Ross, 1898*

The array of shipping to be frequently seen at Tanjong Pagar and Borneo Wharves gives the first impression of the real importance of Singapore. Here are nearly two miles of steamers, in an unbroken row, and it is not uncommon to see these ships "double banked" or even three deep on occasion. The graving docks are full of steamers, while there are other vessels waiting in the roads until they can get a berth at the wharves. Steam tugs and cargo boats block up the sea front, while on shore swarms of coolies are working coals and merchandise under a blazing hot sun, as if their very lives depended on their efforts.

The Magnificently Oriental Watering Cart

From The White Man's Rule in Singapore *by Poultney Bigelow, 1899*

We passed a stretch of road that was being newly macadamized. The steam-roller was of the most approved English make. The watering cart was drawn by little white bullocks, and driven by Malays with turbans. It seemed to take five Malays to do this driving. One roosted aloft on top of the barrel for the purpose of controlling the outgo of water. He seemed very proud of his appointment. Another native in a big turban roosted on the pole and controlled the little cattle. Evidently the man who drove was not allowed to control the water also. Then there was a man in thin brown legs and much turban who walked solemnly behind, enjoying a foot-bath on the Kneippcure plan. He was obviously a government functionary, though his exact sphere of usefulness I could not discover. He appeared to be something in the nature of a rear-guard. Then there was a fore-loper, or advance-guard, for the purpose of clearing the way. There appeared to be the idea that the little bullocks might suddenly go mad and rush ahead; at any rate, it gave congenial employment to one more native, and that was something. There was yet another, who bent down now and then to pick up a piece of stone or brush away some irregularity unseen by ordinary eyes. This outfit was a treat to me. It was solemn; it was full of self-consciousness, it was magnificently Oriental. Every man about that water-cart bore upon his shoulders the full responsibilities of British prestige in the Far East. I have seen men in sublime moments. I have seen the red-capped station-master of Germany strut up and down his platform when an imperial train is about to arrive; but even that impressed me less than the watering-cart of Singapore with its municipal hierarchy of Malay ministers, each one earning perhaps two cents per day.

Singapore's Bearded Guardians

The first Sikhs to arrive at Singapore were policemen or soldiers recruited in the Punjab. Later, Sikh men arrived independently and found work as guards, or *jagas* in Malay. Singapore was a place to earn money you spent at home, so long stays were rare, but the *jagas* - tall, distinctively dressed and of a martial people - slowly rose in real as well as symbolic importance. They were hired as the doormen of large hotels and, in a society that was for many years lawless, as the bodyguards of important men, both Chinese and European. The Chinese burnt *jaga* effigies and erected statues of the men - all surnamed Singh (lion) - beside the more traditional stone lions guarding their tombs.

"The Sikhs are splendid fellows, not a man under 6ft., and they are drilled like soldiers, and are armed with Sniders—being, in fact, a sort of military police, which supplements the European and Malay contingents of the Singapore police-force."

The Brisbane Courier, *Aug 30, 1884*

Clod-Hopping Beetle Crushers

From Records and Recollections *(1889–1934) by John Henry Matthew Robson*

There is one thing a policeman does not like, that is his boots. I should be very sorry to have to wear them myself when new, even if I were paid for doing so. Patience—patience, and as the years roll on somebody with a little originality may yet be able to obtain a light strong boot fit alike for Sikhs and Malays, and so abolish the present heavy cumbersome clod-hopping beetle-crushers.

Propitiating the Joss

From Arnold Wright & H.A. Cartwright's Twentieth Century Impressions of British Malaya, *1908*

In the Chinese joss-houses one of the things that strike the European visitor as most curious is the way in which edible offerings are made to the "joss." A Chinese lady, resplendent in silks and jewellery, will come along, perhaps bearing a huge basket replete with all sorts of delicacies, prominent among which are roasted ducks and coloured Chinese cakes. After the necessary formalities have been gone though, the edibles are duly placed out in festal array in front of the particular "joss" whom it is sought to propitiate. Then the worshipper burns some joss-sticks and coloured papers, after which the coolie sweeps all the good things back into the basket and the party go off rejoicing to feast upon them at home.

"One morning I "did" the Chinese temple. The building was of the usual kind, profusely ornamented with porcelain flowers, &c., and bristling with prickly dragons. The chief objects of interest were several frightfully ugly idols sitting in state. No sort of worship was proceeding; indeed, the temple seemed more of a show than anything else, and our guide took us round with a grin on his face not at all suggestive of reverence."

The Brisbane Courier, *Apr 10, 1875*

The Cathay Building

The Cathay was Singapore's first skyscraper and, at 83.5m (16 floors), the tallest building on the island until 1958. Opened in Oct 1939, its previously unknown luxuries - including an air-conditioned cinema, with armchairs - had Singapore's high society chattering until the Japanese occupied the building in 1942 and turned it into the headquarters of their Broadcasting Department, Propaganda Department and Military Information Bureau. The Cathay was also used as accommodation for senior officers and the heads of executed Singaporeans were displayed outside, stuck on poles. The Cathay was used as a headquarters again when the British returned, this time by Lord Admiral Louis Mountbatten's South East Asia Command.

The Cathay Building in 1958

A Queen is Crowned

A description of Queen Elizabeth II's Coronation in 1953, from The Rose of Singapore *by Peter Neville*

The citizens of the tiny British colonial island of Singapore celebrated this once-in-a-lifetime event in spectacular style. Boldly, and with great reverence to their new monarch, they transformed the already gay and colourful city into one bedecked with Union Jack's and buntings, red, white and blue streamers and banners, millions of glittering, coloured lights and countless jewelled crowns all painted gold...In brightly illuminated shopfronts the message 'Long Live the Queen' was splashed across banners in red upon gold displaying the peoples' respect and goodwill towards their new ruler. On this day no talk was heard of independence. In honour of the Coronation, Singapore's rich diversity of ethnic groups united as one to celebrate this day joyously and with devotion towards the island's new ruler. The British, Chinese, Indians and Malays were all her subjects, she their ruler...Mounted on the roof of the tallest building in Singapore, the newly opened Cathay Building, was a brightly-illuminated crown, where, immediately below the crown, a brightly-lit, intricately designed royal coach drawn by four horses moved clockwise electronically around the top of the building. And below, at the Cathay Theatre, the words 'A Queen is Crowned' shone from thousands of clear, brilliant electric lights.

A Street Scene

In The Otago Witness, *May 1, 1901*

Outside in the roads all is noise and motion. At one point by the roadside a seller of abominable sweet-stuffs drives a thriving trade which calls for an immense expenditure of vituperation and expletive. Close at hand a street barber has pitched his portable shop and is calmly engaged in shaving the head of a fellow Chinaman whose face is wrapped with the luxury of his sensations. A dozen Chinese pedlars stroll through the crowd shaking their wares with voices like those of disconsolate dogs. Groups of coolies walk along staring at nothing particular; others trip and shamble beneath double loads suspended across their shoulders at either end of stout sticks.

> "If there is a Chinese terrestrial paradise, this is where it is to be found. Amongst them it is an accepted fiction that the territory of the Straits Settlements is part of China, and a place where good Confucians may pass their lives and leave their bones."
>
> *Walter Del Mar,* Around the World through Japan, *1904*

Chinese Theatrics

From The Manners and Customs of the Chinese of the Straits Settlements *by J.D. Vaughan, 1879*

In the front of the temples is a large flagged square surrounded by a high wall, in which temporary stages are erected for theatrical performances; when of course the place is crowded by worshippers who are attracted more by them, than the service of the gods. Chinese gods appear to be particularly fond of the drama. The wise say that these performances are often given to screen gamblers who play in adjoining houses, whilst the attention of the police is attracted to the crowd before the theatre.

1c
1c
STRAITS SETTLEMENTS
1c
1c
STRAITS SETTLEMENTS
1c
1c
STRAITS SETTLEMENTS

Fire Walking

From Chinese Joy; Hindu Ritual *by W.G.B., Oct 18, 1941*

At the chief Hindu temple in Singapore, thirty or forty Hindus of all ages, who had more than unduly sinned, purified their souls by marching through a pit of white hot ashes with naked feet…In the centre of the courtyard stood a great heap of white-hot ashes, from which deep red flames shot up as attendants, with long-handled rakes, spread them across the base of the foot-deep pit, about 30 feet long by 15 wide. The heat was so fierce that bowls of water were continually poured over the coals… To the accompaniment of terrific shouting, a black goat was led in, and after a couple of buckets of water had been poured over it to purify it, and some passes had been made with a white cloth, its head was severed from its body with one terrific blow from a scimitar wielded by a half-naked temple priest. The body was seized by the hind legs and quickly dragged twice round the glowing pit of ashes. By this time the excitement grew to such a pitch that huge, bearded Sikhs intervened, using the thongs end of their batons to quieten the surging mass… A team of drummers next entered the arena, and, squatting down at a respectful distance from the coals, commenced a thrum-thrum-thrum on deep skin drums. More shouts and cries, then a figure, naked from the waist up, with long hair hanging round his face, a saffron-colored middle, and a garland of flowers swinging round his neck, burst through a crowd of attendants at the far end of the arena. For a moment he stood, green leaves held in his clasped hands, high above his head, whilst a priest slashed at his arms with a rope thong. Then he stepped into the coals, walking the first few yards steadily; then, bounding across and jumping into and out of the pool of water, he fell into the arms of waiting attendants...One after another, others followed him, some with green leaves clasped in their mouths, others with long pins thrust though top and bottom lips, to stop them crying out.

"Satai"

From Return to Malaya *by R.H. Bruce Lockhart, 1936*

"Satai," I said. "I want eat 'Satai.'" I dipped a tooth-pick into an imaginary dish and raised an imaginary piece of meat to my mouth. The puller grinned and set off at a steady trot until we came to a narrow street close to the sea. Here, occupying various pitches like the men who sell hot Frankfurter sausages in the vegetable market in Prague, were the Malay "Satai" cooks…I got out and went over to an empty stall kept by a plump Malay gentleman, who obviously enjoyed his own cooking. He had a couple of boxes set on end. On one of them he had a small charcoal fire. On the other were the various dishes containing respectively a curry, too hot for the uninitiated, a milder curry, and a delicious kind of onion sauce.

"Satai, Tuan?" he asked and, when I nodded, he began the ritual. With a small straw-plaited fan he began to stir the charcoal to a bright flame. While it burnt he chopped up onion and cucumber on a plate. When the fire was at the proper glow, he produced from his box pieces of chicken meat fixed on little sticks in much the same way as the Russians prepare "shashlyk." Then, dipping the sticks of meat into a can of fat, he grilled them for several minutes on his fire. He bowed. The "Satai" were ready.

A Chinese rice cake seller

A Strange Spectacle

From The Critic in the Orient by George Hamlin Fitch, 1913

The most conspicuous places of business on these streets were the large restaurants, where hundreds of Chinese were eating their chow at small tables. The din was terrific, and the lights flashing on the naked yellow skins, wet with perspiration, made a strange spectacle. Next to these eating houses in number were handsomely decorated places in which Chinese women plied the most ancient trade known to history. Some of these women were very comely, but few were finely dressed, as in this quarter cheapness seemed to be the rule in everything. Around some of these places crowds of Chinese gathered and exchanged comment apparently on attractive new arrivals in these resorts of vice. Many of the inmates were young girls, fourteen or sixteen years old.

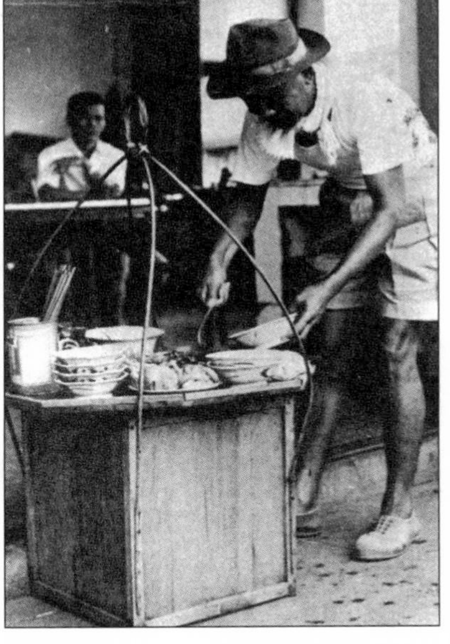

'There was said to be a great number of tigers on the island and some hundreds of Chinamen were reported to be killed each year by them, but as the Chinamen belonged to secret societies who were in perpetual feud and always ready to kill each other, I am afraid that many a murder has been falsely attributed to the "gentleman in stripes."'

General Douglas Hamilton, 1892

An early advertisement for tiger balm.

Shopping for Tigers

From Trapping Wild Animals in Malay Jungles *by Charles Mayer, 1921*

A few days after we arrived at Singapore, Gaylord said: "Do you want to come with me while I buy some animals?" Naturally, I jumped at the chance. We went to the house of Mahommed Ariff, the Malay dealer...He was squatted in the center of his courtyard, surrounded by cages containing the animals brought in from the jungle by his native agents. He was a wicked old devil and a man had only to glance at him to be convinced of the fact. His forebears...were pirates, and he was the chief of a clique of Samgings (the native gangsters), composed of natives who would commit any crime he ordered. It was by using such methods that he held his monopoly of the animal business; the natives were afraid of him, and no European or native had dared to interfere with his trade. His head was shaven and his lips and chin were stained crimson from chewing betel-nut. He had little bullet eyes, set in a fat face. My impression of Mahommed Ariff was that he would be a bad man to have as an enemy...His religion was "to do all Europeans," but he could not help being honest with us...That day we bought a tiger, several monkeys and a pair of leopards.

The Little Attendant

In A Visit to the Indian Archipelago *by Capt. Henry Keppel, 1852*

Not long ago, as a Malayan boy, who was employed by his parents in herding some water-buffaloes, was driving his charge home by the borders of the jungle, a tiger made a sudden spring, and, seizing the lad by the thigh, was dragging him off, when two old bull buffaloes, hearing the shriek of distress from the well-known voice of their little attendant, turned round and charged with their usual rapidity. The tiger, thus closely pressed, was obliged to drop his prey, to defend himself. While one buffalo fought and successfully drove the tiger away, the other kept guard over the wounded boy. Later in the evening, when the anxious father, alarmed, came out with attendants to seek his child, he found that the whole herd, with the exception of the two old buffaloes, had dispersed themselves to feed, but that they were still there – one standing over the bleeding body of their little friend, while the other kept watch at the edge of the jungle for the return of the tiger.

The Commandos of Communism

British rubber planters and tin miners in Malaya were not insured against war, so the Malayan Emergency, fought from 1948 to 1960, was never officially labelled as such. Graham Greene, in a 1951 article titled "Malaya, the Forgotten War" was not similarly constrained.

The nature of this war has been little understood abroad. It is not a nationalist war; 95% of the enemy combatants are Chinese and of the few Malays in the jungle the greater part are Indonesian terrorists...Our British consciences can be clear—we are not holding down Malaya: we are fighting a straightforward war against Communism and its Chinese adherents, and it is a more serious war than the use in the press of the word bandit suggests. Bandits could not year after year survive the hard jungle life as these men do: a few thousand bandits could not continue to operate against 100,000 troops. These men are the commandos of Communism, organized like a Russian division, with their political branches, their educational branches, their political commissars, their tireless and industrious intelligence service. No one knows where their GHQ lies—perhaps in one of the cities, Singapore, Kuala Lumpur, perhaps even in the old and relatively peaceful city of Malacca—but the leader is known. He fought the Japanese in World War II and marched in the Victory Parade in London...But you cannot measure the enemy's strength only by the few thousand fighters who emerge from the jungle to shoot up a car or a patrol, to murder a planter, to derail a train. Their strength is estimated at between 3,000 and 5,000. In this dense country one numbers casualties on the fingers—the death of a dozen Communists is a major victory and they have no difficulty in acquiring new members. Their real strength lies in the unarmed combatants of the ground organization known as the Min Yuen. Here we are on speculative ground, but it is unlikely that this organization runs into less than six figures. Its main responsibility is supply, but it is employed also for intelligence, propaganda and liaison work, and it is responsible—perhaps that is its chief success—for the suspicion which rises everywhere like the mist from the saturated Malayan soil. Don't mention what time you are leaving on the telephone—the operator may be a member of the Min Yuen. Don't talk about your movements in front of your waiter or your room boy. Do you remember that young resettlement officer they killed last month? He told his Chinese taxi girl where he was going next day.

> "Before I left for Malaya I had been advised not to refer to the operations as 'war,' but as 'the emergency,' and to the Malayan Liberation Army as 'bandits.' It did not take me long to find out that the so-called bandits were a well-trained, highly disciplined and skilfully led force."
>
> *James Griffiths,* Pages from Memory, *1969*

A Communist soldier

> "While the whole world becomes excited over whether war is on or off in Korea, the forgotten war in Malaya goes on. There is the daily trip of casualties: 400 civilians had been killed in the first 11 months of last year, one guerrilla camp destroyed, one surrendered, three guerrillas shot and six escaped. the war is like a mist; it pervades everything; it saps the spirits; it won't clear."
>
> *Graham Greene, 1951*

REWARDS

for information

Substantial **REWARDS** will be paid to all who co-operate with the authorities in providing information about Intimidators and Gangsters.

The source of all information given to the Police is kept Secret.

Up to **$2,000** have been paid to a person who has given useful Information.

Communicate with the Police by every means possible.

Useful Information

EARNS

CASH

Government Press, Kuala Lumpur.

EMERGENCY REGULATIONS

are

NOW IN FORCE

HOW DO THEY AFFECT

YOU?

VOTE FOR ALTERNATIVE "A" ON REFERENDUM DAY

THE SINGAPORE NATIONAL REFERENDUM ORDINANCE 1962
(No. 19 OF 1962)
SECTION 18.

A	Saya sokong perchantuman yang memberikan kapada Singapura kuasa otonomi dalam perkara buroh, pelajaran dan perkara2 lain yang di-persetujui, sabagaimana yang terkandong dalam Kertas Perentah No. 33, Tahun 1961, dan dengan sendiri-nya warganegara2 Singapura menjadi warganegara2 Malaysia. I support merger giving Singapore autonomy in labour, education and other agreed matters as set out in Command Paper No. 33 of 1961, with Singapore citizens automatically becoming citizens of Malaysia.	Bendera Negara Singapura Singapore State Flag	X
B	Saya sokong perchantuman penoh yang tidak bersharat bagi Singapura sa-bagai negeri yang sama taraf-nya dengan sa-belas buah Negeri2 Bahagian menurut sharat2 Perlembagaan Persekutuan Tanah Melayu. I support complete and unconditional merger for Singapore as a state on an equal basis with the other eleven states in accordance with the Constitutional documents of the Federation of Malaya.	Bendera Negeri Pulau Pinang Penang State Flag	
C	Saya sokong penyertaan Singapura ka-dalam Malaysia dengan sharat2 yang tidak kurang daripada sharat2 yang di-berikan kapada wilayah2 Borneo. I support Singapore entering Malaysia on terms no less favourable than those given to the Borneo territories.	Lambang2 atas bendera Sabah dan Sarawak Badges on the Flags of North Borneo and Sarawak	

VOTE FOR OUR OWN SINGAPORE FLAG – THE SYMBOL OF ALTERNATIVE "A"

VOTE FOR MERGER WITH SPECIAL RIGHTS!

VOTE FOR EQUALITY FOR OUR FOUR LANGUAGES!

VOTE FOR OUR OWN CONTROL OVER EDUCATION!

VOTE FOR OUR OWN LABOUR POLICY!

VOTE FOR A COMMON CITIZENSHIP!

VOTE FOR AUTOMATIC CONVERSION TO MALAYSIAN CITIZENSHIP!

On Sept. 1, 1962, Singapore held a referendum on its merger with Malaysia. The ballot had three options, but none allowed a vote against the merger, despite strong objections from Barisan Sosialis – a leftwing breakaway from the People's Action Party. This poster, an example ballot with a cross beside Option A, led to accusations that the government was going to distribute marked ballots. It didn't, and because Barisan Sosialis encouraged people to submit blank ballots in protest, many remained unmarked. The government counted these as in favour of Option A, which obtained 73% of the vote.

Love in any Language

From Beds in the East, *1959, in Anthony Burgess's Malayan Trilogy*

'It's difficult to say these things in Malay…And in Chinese, too.' He sucked the lip of the brimming coffee-cup. 'Some things the British brought with them. Along with their language.' His brow let the kerosene lamp etch out the puzzle. '*Love,*' he said. 'Do you know that word? *Love, love. I love you*. In Mandarin we say: "*Wo ai ni.*" But it's not the same.'

'I know that,' said Syed Hassan. 'I *love you*. It's on the films. Then they *kiss*.' He used the English word; the Malay word *chium* meant to plough the beloved's face with one's nose: it was not the same thing, despite the dictionaries…

'I'm in love,' said Robert Loo in English. He burst out with it; he had to tell someone. 'That's why I've got to go back home, you see. I'm in love. Everything...' He paused, juggling in his mind with Malay and English; the English words fell into his hand. 'Everything *feels* different.'

…Syed Hassan felt envy. That was an experience he still had not had; he felt bitter because the whole thing seemed so typical: the Chinese cutting out the Malays even in that particular business. But, in the act of formulating the words of resentment, he remembered his father. Race, race, race – his father's dinner-table theme. The Tamils had done this to him, and the Sikhs had done that, and the Chinese were pig-guzzling infidels, and as for the British...

"A gang of half-educated, swollen headed, power-mad adolescent demagogues trying to take over the country. I told them many facts which, as self-claimed leaders, they should have known but did not. What they were really trying to carry out boiled down to nothing but a gigantic swindle."

C. C. Too, SRC President of Raffles College, referring to leaders of the Malayan Communist Party, 1941

A British psyops leaflet dropped on Malayan guerrillas, describing the "Qualifications of a High Ranking Officer".

A Moment of Anguish

Singapore was expelled from the Federation of Malaysia on Aug 9, 1965. Later that day, Prime Minister Lee Kuan Yew gave a press conference, during which he famously broke down in tears.

We must survive. We have a right to survive. And, to survive, we must be sure that we cannot be just over-run…Singapore, as proclaimed by myself on behalf of the people and Government of Singapore today is an independent, sovereign nation with a will and a capacity of its own...If Singapore could have been governed by the gun indefinitely without breaking whoever tries to do it, you know, either financially or militarily, I think it would have been tried – either by the British before instead of granting independence and Merger and Malaysia, or I think by us, or by the former Central Government. I think everybody understands that…Any other kind of Malaysia than a Malaysian Malaysia is unacceptable…Well, perhaps now with Singapore out there could be a Malaysia because the process would be much slower, will be much more gradual. The impetus of a highly-urbanised and a politically sophisticated city and 2-million people in it maybe set a pace which was too – well, which they thought was too fierce…For me it is a moment of anguish because all my life... you see, the whole of my adult life...I have believed in Merger and the unity of these two territories. You know, it's a people, connected by geography, economics, and ties of kinship...Would you mind if we stop for a while…

[The recording stopped for 20 minutes, while the P.M. regained his composure.]

Just as a river loops and bends around mountains and valleys before it reaches the sea, so the history of a people takes many loops and bends before it reaches its destiny…Nobody in Singapore at this present moment and for the next five maybe ten years, can ever persuade Singapore to go back into Malaysia after our experience. But somebody will do it one day, perhaps in a different form, under different circumstances…We are going to have a multi-racial nation in Singapore. We will set the example. This is not a Malay nation; this is not a Chinese nation; this is not an Indian nation. Everybody will have his place: equal; language, culture, religion. We could not achieve multi-racialism and integration in Malaysia. But we will achieve it in Singapore. We have all learnt our lessons.

SEPARATION
SINGAPORE'S INDEPENDENCE ON 9th AUGUST 1965
"Singapore shall be forever a sovereign, democratic and independent nation, founded upon the principles of liberty and justice"

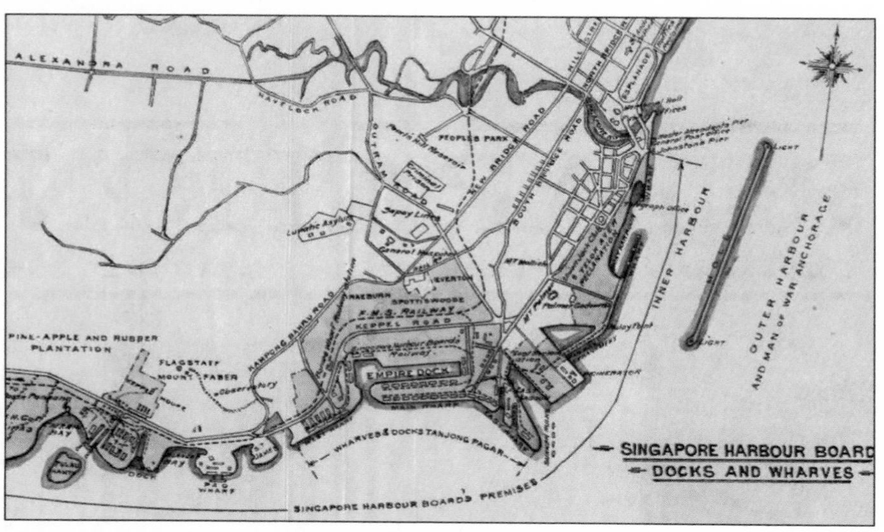
ALEXANDRA ROAD
HAVELOCK ROAD
OUTRAM ROAD
PEOPLES PARK
NEW BRIDGE ROAD
SOUTH BRIDGE ROAD
NORTH BRIDGE ROAD
HILL STREET
ESPLANADE
INNER HARBOUR
OUTER HARBOUR AND MAN OF WAR ANCHORAGE
MOLE
LIGHT
Lunatic Asylum
Sepoy Lines
EVERTON
SPOTTISWOODE
F.M.S. RAILWAY
KEPPEL ROAD
KAMPONG BAHRU ROAD
PINE-APPLE AND RUBBER PLANTATION
FLAGSTAFF
MOUNT FABER
EMPIRE DOCK
MAIN WHARF
WHARVES & DOCKS TANJONG PAGAR
INCINERATOR
SINGAPORE HARBOUR BOARD
DOCKS AND WHARVES
SINGAPORE HARBOUR BOARDS PREMISES

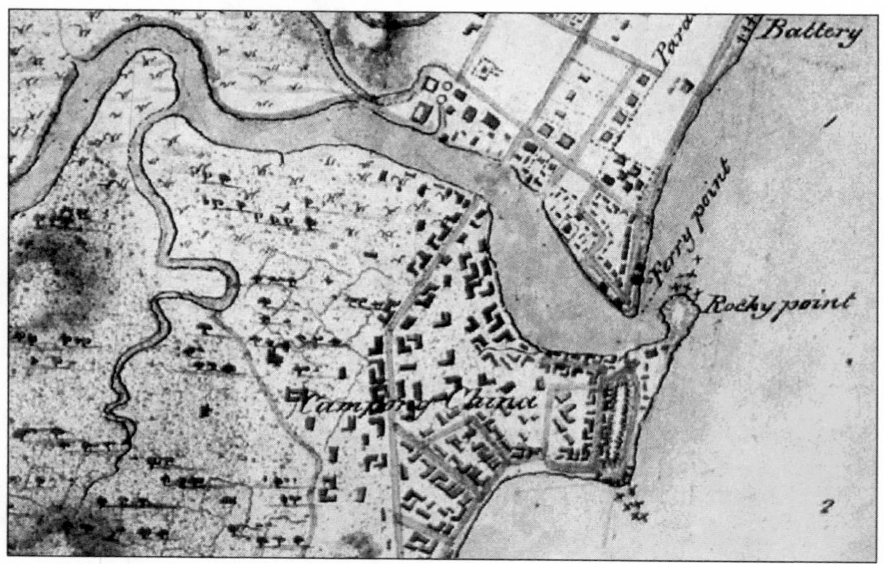
Battery
Ferry point
Rocky point
Kampong China

Bibliography

Bengal Civilian. *Rambles in Java and the Straits in 1852*. Singapore: Oxford UP, 1987.

Bigelow, Poultney. "The White Man's Rule in Singapore." *Harper's*. Web. 23 Feb. 2010. <http://www.harpers.org/archive/1900/02/0003472>.

Bin, Abdul Kadir, Abdullah. *The Hikayat Abdullah*. Trans. A. H. Hill. Kuala Lumpur: Oxford Univ., 1970.

Bird, Isabella Lucy. *The Golden Chersonese and the Way Thither*. London: J. Murray, 1883.

Boulger, Demetrius. *The Life of Sir Stamford Raffles*. London: H. Marshall, 1897.

Braddon, Russell. *The Naked Island*. Garden City, N.Y.: Doubleday, 1953.

Brassey, Annie Allnutt. *A Voyage in the "Sunbeam": Our Home on the Ocean for Eleven Months*. Chicago: Belford, Clarke, 1881.

The Brisbane Courier. 10 Apr. 1875: Pg. 5. 26 Mar. 1884: Pg. 5. 30 Aug. 1884: Pg. 3.

Brooke, James. *The Private Letters of Sir James Brooke, K.C.B, Rajah of Sarwak*. Gardners, 2007.

Brown, Cecil. "Malay Jungle War." *LIFE* 12 Jan. 1942: 32-38. *Google Books*. Web. 2 Mar. 2010.

Brown, Edwin A. *Indiscreet Memories*. London: Kelly & Walsh, 1935.

Buckley, Charles Burton. *An Anecdotal History of Old times in Singapor*. Singapore: Fraser & Neave, 1902.

Burgess, Anthony. *Beds in the East*. London: Heinemann, 1959.

Cameron, Charlotte Wales-Almy. *Wanderings in South-eastern Seas,*. Boston: Small, Maynard, and, 1924.

Cameron, John. *Our Tropical Possessions in Malayan India*. London: Smith, Elder, 1865.

Carnegie, Andrew. *Round the World*. New York: Scribner, 1884.

Cavenagh, Orfeur. *Reminiscences of an Indian Official*. London: W. H. Allen, 1884.

Churchill, Winston. *The Hinge of Fate*. Boston: Houghton Mifflin, 1950.

Clavell, James. *King Rat, a Novel*. Boston: Little, Brown, 1962.

Clifford, Hugh Charles. *In a Corner of Asia; Being Tales and Impressions of Men and Things in the Malay Peninsula*. London: T.F. Unwin, 1899.

Conrad, Joseph, Frederick Robert Karl, Laurence Davies, and Owen Knowles. *The Collected Letters of Joseph Conrad*. Cambridge: Cambridge UP, 2002.

Conrad, Joseph. *Lord Jim: a Sketch*. Edinburgh: W. Blackwood & Sons, 1899.

Conrad, Joseph. *Youth and Two Other Stories*. New York: McClure, Phillips, 1903.

Cook, John Angus Bethune. *Sunny Singapore an Account of the Place and Its People, with a Sketch of the Results of Missionary Work*. London: Stock, 1907.

Coupland, Reginald. *Raffles, 1781-1826*. London: Oxford UP, 1926.

Coward, Noel. *Present Indicative*. Garden City, N.Y.: Doubleday, Doran and, 1937.

Dare, G.M. *Accounts of Singapore Life*, 1856. Collected in *Travellers' Tales of Old Singapore*. Ed. Michael Wise. Singapore: Marshall Cavendish Editions, 2008.

Times Special Correspondent, *On the Empire Trail*, 1921. Collected in *Travellers' Tales of Old Singapore*. Ed. Michael Wise. Singapore: Marshall Cavendish Editions, 2008.

Davidson, G. F. *Trade and Travel in the Far East; Or, Recollections of Twenty-one Years Passed in Java, Singapore, Australia, and China*. London: Madden, 1846.

Del, Mar Walter. *Around the World through Japan,*. London: A. and C. Black, 1904.

D.I.N. *Singapore Jottings*. Singapore: Koh Yew Hean, 1885.

Dixon, Alec. *Singapore Patrol,*. London [etc.: G.G. Harrap &, 1935.

Ellms, Charles. *The Pirates Own Book, Or, Authentic Narratives of the Lives Exploits, and Executions of the Most Celebrated Sea Robbers*. Boston: T. Groom, 1837.

"An Era of Empire Ends at Singapore." *LIFE* 23 Feb. 1942: 17-21. *Google Books*. Web. 21 Feb. 2010.

Fairlie, John. *Life in the Malay Peninsula*. Singapore: J. Fairlie, 1892.

Fitch, George Hamlin. *The Critic in the Orient*. San Francisco: P. Elder &, 1913.

Foran, W. Robert. *Malayan Symphony; Being the Impressions Gathered during a Six Months' Journey through the Straits Settlements, Federated Malay States, Siam, Sumatra, Java and Bali*. London: Hutchinson &, 1935.

Fraser, George MacDonald. *Flashman's Lady: from the Flashman Papers, 1842-1845*. London: Barrie & Jenkins, 1977.

Frost, Mark Ravinder., and Yu-Mei Balasingamchow. *Singapore: a Biography*. Hong Kong: Hong Kong UP, 2009.

Gammans, Leonard David. *Singapore Sequel,*. London: Signpost, 1944.

Greene, Graham. "Malaya, the Forgotten War." *LIFE* 30 July 1951. *Google Books*. Web.

Griffith, James. *Pages from Memory*. London: Dent, 1969.

Hahn, Emily. *Raffles of Singapore, a Biography*. Garden City, New York: Doubleday & Company, 1946.

Hamilton, Alexander. *A New Account of the East Indies*. Edinburgh: J. Mosman, 1727.

Hamilton, Douglas, and Edward Hamilton. *Records of Sport in Southern India*. London: R.H. Porter, 1892.

Hendley, Charles M. *Trifles of Travel,*. Washington, 1924.

Hill, Samuel Charles. *Episodes of Piracy in the Eastern Seas, 1519 to 1851*. Bombay: Printed at the British India, 1920.

Hornaday, William T. *Two Years in the Jungle: the Experiences of a Hunter and Naturalist in India, Ceylon, the Malay Peninsula and Borneo*. New York: Charles Scribner's Sons, 1885.

"Japanese PSYOP During WWII." Web. 31 Mar. 2010. <http://www.psywarrior.com/JapanPSYOPWW2b.html>.

Keppel, Henry. *A Sailor's Life under Four Sovereigns*. London: Macmillan, 1899.

Keppel, Henry. *A Visit to the Indian Archipelago*.

Keppel, Henry, and James Brooke. *A Visit to the Indian Archipelago*. London: Richard Bentley, 1852.

Ker, David. *Among the Dark Mountains: Or, Cast Away in Sumatra*. London: Blackie, 1907.

Kipling, Rudyard, and Rudyard Kipling. *The Seven Seas*. Toronto: G.N. Morang, 1900.

Kipling, Rudyard. *From Sea to Sea*. New York: Appleton, 1899.

LaMotte, Ellen N. *The Ethics of Opium*. New York & London: Century, 1924.

Lane, Edward G. *Letters Written to my Children*, 1931.Collected in *Travellers' Tales of Old Singapore*. Ed. Michael Wise. Singapore: Marshall Cavendish Editions, 2008.

Lee, Kuan Yew. *The Singapore Story: Memoirs of Lee Kuan Yew*. Singapore: Simon & Schuster, 1998.

Li, Chung Chu. *A Description of Singapore. Travellers' Tales of Old Singapore*. Ed. Michael Wise. Singapore: Marshall Cavendish Editions, 2008.

Lockhart, Robert Hamilton Bruce. *Return to Malaya*. New York: G.P. Putnam's Sons, 1936.

Low, N. I., and H. M. Cheng. *This Singapore: (our City of Dreadful Night)*. Singapore: City Book Store, 1948.

MacCallum, Scott John H. *Eastern Journey*. London: Travel Book Club, 1939.

Makepeace, Walter, Gilbert E. Brooke, and Roland St. John Braddell. *One Hundred Years of Singapore*. London: J. Murray, 1921.

Malcolm, Howard. *Travels in South-eastern Asia: Embracing Hindustan, Malaya, Siam, and China*. Boston: Gould, Kendall and Lincoln, 1839.

Marsden, William. *A Grammar of the Malayan Language*. London: Cox & Baylis, 1812.

Mayer, Charles. *Trapping Wild Animals in Malay Jungles,*. New York: Duffield, 1921.

McNair, John Frederick Adolphus, and W. D. Bayliss. *Prisoners Their Own Warders*. Westminster: Constable, 1899.

Morrell, Benjamin. *A Narrative of Four Voyages*. New York: J. & J. Harper, 1832.

Neville, Peter. *The Rose of Singapore*. Singapore: Monsoon, 2006.

Norman, Henry. *The Peoples and Politics of the Far East; Travels and Studies in the British, French, Spanish and Portuguese Colonies, Siberia, China, Japan, Korea, Siam and Malaya*. New York: Scribner, 1904.

Oldham, William Fitzjames. *Malaysia; Nature's Wonderland*. Cincinnati: Jennings and Graham, 1907.

Oliphant, Laurence. *Narrative of the Earl of Elgin's Mission to China and Japan in the Years 1857-59: with Illustrations from Original Drawings and Photographs*. Edinburgh: Blackwood and Sons, 1859.

Osborn, Sherard. *My Journal in Malayan Waters; Or, the Blockade of Quedah*. London: Routledge, Warne, and Routledge, 1860.

Pearson, Henry C. *What I Saw in the Tropics*. New York: India Rubber Pub., 1904.

Penfield, Frederic Courtland. *East of Suez: Ceylon, India, China and Japan*. New York: Century, 1899.

Pfeifer, Ida Reyer. *A Lady's Second Journey round the World*. London: Longman, Brown, Green & Longmans, 1855.

Pickering, Charles, and John Charles Hall. *The Races of Man, and Their Geographical Distribution*. London: H.G. Bohn, 1854.

Pickering, William. "Chinese Secret Societies, Part I." *Journal of the Straits Branch of the Royal Asiatic Society* (1878): 63-84.

Pickering, William. *Little Short of Slavery*, 1877. Collected in *Travellers' Tales of Old Singapore*. Ed. Michael Wise. Singapore: Marshall Cavendish Editions, 2008.

Powell, E. Alexander. *Where the Strange Trails Go Down*. New York: C. Scribner's Sons, 1921.

Raffles, Stamford. "On the Advantages of Affording the Means of Education to the Inhabitants of the Further East." Ed. W.B. Collyer. *The Investigator* (1821). *Google Books*. Web. 07 July 2010.

Read, W. H. *Play and Politics: Recollections of Malaya*. London: Wells, Gardner, Darton, 1901.

Redfern, James. *Looking for Luck*, 1930. Collected in *Travellers' Tales of Old Singapore*. Ed. Michael Wise. Singapore: Marshall Cavendish Editions, 2008.

Reith, G. M. *Handbook to Singapore: with Map and a Plan of the Botanic Gardens*. Singapore: Singapore and Straits Office, 1892.

Rennie, James Stuart Macready. *Musings of J.S.M.R., Mostly Malayan*. Singapore: Malaya Pub. House, 1933.

Robson, J. H. M. *People in a Native State*. Singapore: Printed at the Singapore and Straits Printing Office, and Published by Walter Makepeace, 1894.

Robson, John Henry Matthew. *Records and Recollections (1889-1934),*. Kuala Lumpur, F.M.S.: Kyle, Palmer &, 1934.

Ross, John Dill. *The Capital of a Little Empire: a Descriptive Study of a British Crown Colony in the Far East*. Singapore: Kelly & Walsh, 1898.

"A Scene in Singapore." *Otago Witness* 1 May 1901, Issue 2459 ed.: 64. *Papers Past*. Web. 19 Nov. 2009. <http://paperspast.natlib.govt.nz/>.

Scott, Charles Payson Gurley. *The Malayan Words in English*. New Haven, Conn., U.S.A.: American Oriental Society, 1897.

Shellabear, William Girdlestone. *The Singapore Triglot Vocabulary*. Singapore: American Mission, 1891.

A Short History of the Port of Singapore: with Particular Reference to the Undertakings of the Singapore Harbour Board. Singapore: Fraser & Neave, 1922.

"Singapore: Britain's Far Eastern Fortress." *LIFE* 21 July 1941: 61. *Google Books*. Web. 24 Mar. 2010.

"SINGAPORE: Example for Capitalists." *TIME* 7 Nov. 1960. Web. 10 May 2010. <http://www.time.com/time/magazine/article/0,9171,826695-1,00.html>.

"Singapore Is Modern City." *LIFE* 21 July 1941: 62. Web.

St, John Horace. *The Indian Archipelago; Its History and Present State*. London: Longman, Brown, Green, and Longmans, 1853.

Sweetser, Delight. *One Way round the World*. Indianapolis: Bobbs-Merrill, 1898.

Swettenham, Frank. *British Malaya: an Account of the Origin and Progress of British Influence in Malaya*. London: J. Lane, 1906.

Thomson, J. *The Straits of Malacca, Indo-China and China Or, Ten Years' Travels, Adventures and Residence Abroad*. London: S. Low, Marston, Low, & Searle, 1875.

Thomson, John Turnbull. *Some Glimpses into Life in the Far East*. London: Richardson &, 1864.

Too, C.C. "The War of the Running Dog." *World War 2 Pictures in Color - WW2inColor.com*. Web. 07 July 2010. <http://www.ww2incolor.com/forum/showthread.php?4699-The-War-of-the-Running-Dog&p=100104>.

Train, George Francis. *An American Merchant in Europe, Asia and Australia*. New York: G.P. Putnam &, 1857.

Treacher, W. H. *British Borneo: Sketches of Brunai, Sarawak, Labuan, and North Borneo*. Singapore: Govt. Dept., 1891.

Trocki, Carl A. *Prince of Pirates: the Temenggongs and the Development of Johor and Singapore, 1784-1885*. Singapore: Singapore UP, 1979.

Tsuji, Masanobu. *Singapore: the Japanese Version*. London: Constable and, 1962.

Vaughan, J. D. *The Manners and Customs of the Chinese of the Straits Settlements.* Singapore: Printed at the Mission, 1879.

Verne, Jules, Dora Leigh, and N. ,. D'Anvers. *Celebrated Travels and Travellers.* London: S. Low, Marston, Searle, & Rivington, 1880.

Wallace, Alfred Russel. *The Malay Archipelago, the Land of the Orang-utan and the Bird of Paradise; a Narrative of Travel, with Studies of Man and Nature*. London: Macmillan and, 1869.

Wang, Ta-hai, and Walter Henry Medhurst. *The Chinaman Abroad: An Account of the Malayan Archipelago, Particularly of Java.* London: J. Snow, 1850.

W.G.B. "A Day in Singapore: Chinese Joy; Hindu Ritual." *The Age* 18 Oct. 1941. Web. 11 Nov. 2009.

White, Theodore H. "Singapore: City and Base." *LIFE* 17 Mar. 1941: 17-21. Web.

Wildman, Rounsevelle. *Tales of the Malayan Coast from Penang to the Philippines.* Boston: Lothrop, 1899.

Wilkes, Charles. *Narrative of the United States Exploring Expedition, during the Years 1838, 1839, 1840, 1841, 1842. With Thirteen Maps.* New York: G.P. Putnam, 1856.

Wilkinson, Hugh. *Sunny Lands and Seas: a Voyage in the SS "Ceylon"* London: John Murray, 1883.

Wilson, Earl. "We're Near Equator Papaya For Breakfast." *St. Petersburg Times* 12 Sept. 1951. *Google Archives*. Web. 21 Jan. 2010.

Windsor, George Frederick and Albert Victor. *The Cruise of Her Majesty's Ship "Bacchante": 1879-1882*. London: Macmillan &, 1882.

Wright, Arnold, and H. A. Cartwright. *Twentieth Century Impressions of British Malaya: Its History, People, Commerce, Industries, and Resources;*. London: Lloyd's Greater Britain Pub., 1908.

Ziegele, Otto. *Singapore Diary*, 1886. Collected in *Travellers' Tales of Old Singapore*. Ed. Michael Wise. Singapore: Marshall Cavendish Editions, 2008.

EARNSHAW
BOOKS

Tales of Old Shanghai

by Graham Earnshaw

ISBN: 978-988-17621-1-5

"It was one of the most cosmopolitan places that ever existed, full of growth and speculation, of rogues and adventurers, of color and life."
Gareth Powell

Tales of Old Peking

by Derek Sandhaus

ISBN: 978-988-18154-2-2

"Through every account, whether humorous, awed or scholarly, breathes a sense of wonder."
Adam Williams, author of
The Palace of Heavenly Pleasure

Tales of Old Hong Kong

by Derek Sandhaus

ISBN: 978-988-18667-2-1

"Captures brilliantly the freewheeling atmosphere of old Hong Kong in all its illicit glory."
James Kynge, author of *China Shakes the World*

www.earnshawbooks.com